Praise for *About A Son*

'Shocking, harrowing and sensitive . . . brings their love for Morgan to vivid life. Whitehouse writes in a spare style reminiscent of Gordon Burn'
Observer, Book of the Week

'An astonishing tale of profound love and grief . . . Exceptional . . . as much as it is about his death, it is also a tribute to who Morgan Hehir was, and the memory of his life will live long inside anyone who reads it'
i

'Truly unique and mightily impressive . . . *About A Son* is both moving and terrifying (I couldn't stop thinking about my two young boys as I was reading it), and the institutional failings Colin uncovers are as shocking as his tenacity is inspiring'
Spectator

'*About A Son* is an extraordinary work. Whitehouse's writing is beautiful, his storytelling deft . . . there is also a huge amount of love in this book. It is Hehir's love in the face of unimaginable trauma that elevates *About A Son* into something courageous, something inexplicably hopeful'
Olivia Potts, *TLS*

'The author *might* have invented a new genre of literature here, so unique are the events leading up to the book's publication. Part evidence-led true-crime investigation and part psycho-spiritual communion with the essence of grief itself, *About A Son* is unlike anything you've ever read, I guarantee'
Time Out

'The book that everyone will be talking about this year: a staggering work of honesty, empathy and humanity, wholly unlike anything else you will have read. Whitehouse is a masterful storyteller who builds an intimate, immersive and unflinching portrait of a boy lost to preventable violence and the family who loved him. I found it absolutely compelling from the first word to the last and know I will never forget it'
Terri White, author of *Coming Undone*

'An incredibly compassionate and moving story of loss, grief and enduring love. The portrait of a father's determination and resilience left me filled with both heartache and hope. David Whitehouse is a singularly gifted and deeply compelling writer and this beautiful book opened my eyes to what creative non-fiction can be and do'

Cathy Rentzenbrink, author of *The Last Act of Love*

'A work of such staggering beauty, such sheer, abject dread. My heart ached, and still does, but I'm so glad I read *About A Son*. I'm so glad David Whitehouse wrote this book. It's profoundly intimate and despairingly universal. It's a story of life and loss, and grief and love. It's remarkable'

Chris Whitaker, author of *We Begin at the End*

'I feel very lucky to have read this book. Extraordinary and important . . . a triumph' Adam Kay, author of *This Is Going to Hurt*

'A book of love and grief, and about what justice can and cannot deliver. I shall always remember Morgan and his family'

Sunjeev Sahota, author of *China Room*

'I was utterly floored by the emotional depth of *About A Son* – a book that reaches so deeply into the human experience that to read it is to be forever changed. It is an unflinching examination of grief, a painstaking deconstruction of injustice and a dispatch from the frontiers of the human heart. David Whitehouse has written something of great power and truth. In doing so, he has ensured that Colin Hehir's beloved son, Morgan, and the family's fight for justice will never be forgotten'

Elizabeth Day, author of *How To Fail*

'Profoundly affecting . . . devastating and extraordinary'

Daily Mail Books of the Year

'Astonishing: a raw, powerful account of grief and the search for truth'

Big Issue Books of the Year

'Magnificent . . . You won't come across books this powerful very often in your lifetime' *Strong Words*

David Whitehouse is the award-winning author of three acclaimed novels. His journalism has appeared in the *Guardian*, *Esquire*, *The Times* and many other publications, and he has written extensively for the screen. He is originally from Nuneaton.

About A Son is his first non-fiction book. It was shortlisted for the Gordon Burn Prize.

About A Son

A Father's Search For Truth

David Whitehouse

PHOENIX

First published in Great Britain in 2022 by Phoenix Books
This paperback edition first published in Great Britain in 2023
by Phoenix Books,
an imprint of The Orion Publishing Group Ltd
Carmelite House, 50 Victoria Embankment
London EC4Y 0DZ

An Hachette UK Company

3 5 7 9 10 8 6 4 2

ISBN (Mass Market Paperback) 978 1 4746 2057 4
ISBN (eBook) 978 1 4746 2058 1
ISBN (Audio) 978 1 4746 2068 0

Typeset by Input Data Services Ltd, Bridgwater, Somerset

Printed and bound in Great Britain by Clays Ltd, Elcograf S.p.A.

www.orionbooks.co.uk
www.phoenix-books.co.uk

To Morgan

There's a fountain in the centre of town. Every summer, bored teenagers uphold a mischievous tradition to fill it with bubble bath. The falling water churns the soap until the foam out-swells the fountain's walls and blows through the streets on the breeze. It floats past bemused shoppers, angry market traders and delighted children, who imagine themselves tumbling, as though the whole of Nuneaton is inside the spinning silver drum of a giant washing machine. That it will come out sparkly and new. They're too young to see that which can't be cleaned, the dirt around the edges of a place like this. The stains left on the fabric of a town by its tragedies.

On the evening of 31 October 2015, near the outskirts of Nuneaton town centre less than half a mile from here, twenty-year-old Morgan Hehir was walking through a park with five friends when they were viciously attacked by three strangers. One of them had a knife. Morgan was stabbed to death.

The brutality and senselessness of Morgan's murder shocked the town. It was impossible to live there, or have lived there, and not hear about it. It was impossible not to feel it in your bones when you did.

Though I left Nuneaton in 1999, when I was eighteen, Morgan's life had been lived and taken on the streets of my formative years. He'd worked at the hospital where I was born, and where my mother worked until her retirement. He'd spray-painted graffiti in the park where I misspent my adolescence. He'd been walking between two pubs where I had some of my first underage drinks when he was murdered by a young man who'd once done the same. We never knew one another, Morgan and I, but I'd been him in the past.

I followed the story from afar, through tired eyes on a phone screen late at night as I fed my baby son. Old school friends discussed new developments on Facebook. Some knew of the young man who lost his life, others the people who took it. My mother would mention his name when we spoke.

'How could they do something so wicked?' she would say, about the killers. It was a question to which no answer ever came.

A little over four years after Morgan's death, in January 2020, I received an email from Claire Harrison, a reporter on the *Nuneaton News*. I'd been friends with Claire since primary school; we were fixtures at each other's childhood birthday parties. She had covered Morgan's murder, the trial of his killers, and his father Colin Hehir's tireless search for the truth about the individual and systemic failures that led to his son's death. As a result, she'd become friends with Colin, who had recently sent her an extraordinary document.

The day after finding out Morgan had been murdered, and motivated only by the desire not to forget a single detail of the ordeal he and his family were about to endure, Colin experienced a remarkable moment of clarity in the thick fog of sorrow. He began to take notes. He'd never written anything longer than a shopping list before, but now he had 164 pages amounting to a diary of events that, in the opening paragraph, promised to 'tell you about the shit we have been through . . . tell the story of what happened'.

Colin wanted Claire's opinion on what he should do with his diary. He wanted as many people to know Morgan's story as possible. Should he post it online? Self-publish it? Would anyone even be interested, or had he lost his mind? Claire wasn't sure. But she offered to send the document to me on the basis that I'd written some books, that I knew the town, and that I may have some ideas.

The truth was, I didn't. I'd never read anything like it before. Colin's diary was a unique record of grief, told from a place deep within it. Of what happens to a parent when a child is taken from them in such sudden, terrible and tragic circumstances. Of how a family picks up the broken pieces and puts itself back together, but only ever in the wrong shape. Of how ordinary people live lives made anything but ordinary by the explosive violence of a young man with a knife. Of how so many families suffer such senseless loss we never hear about. And of how the systems designed to protect us will contort to protect themselves when they fail.

It was a report from the front line of loss. Rough, angry, moving, tender, maddening and blindingly honest, a testament not just to his son's life, but Colin's refusal to give up until he discovered the truth of how Morgan's murder came to be – a murder that should never have taken place.

Though utterly compelling, Colin's diary was intensely personal, overwhelmingly raw and indescribably sad. It was sometimes difficult to read, sometimes impossible. What advice could I give to someone who'd known such pain about what to do with it? As a father of sons, what could I say to a man who had lost one? I wasn't even sure how to begin the conversation. And so, to my shame, I didn't have it. I put the file in a folder I told myself I'd return to, and promised

I'd call Colin when I knew what to say. But though his story didn't leave my mind, that day never arrived.

It was three months later, on 15 April 2020, when I received a message from Colin directly, politely and patiently asking for my gut feelings on what he called his ramblings. It was then that I read his diary again, and we began to talk. Slowly, a way of telling his family's story, in the hope it never happens to another, began to take shape.

That diary and those conversations became the backbone of this book, which also uses interviews, news articles, police reports, reportage and other materials to tell the story of his son, his family, and this time. I will always be honoured that Colin and his family – his wife Sue, and their sons Connor and Eamon – trusted me with his writings, with their experience, and with their pain. I hope only to have done justice to them, and to Morgan.

Loss

Saturday, 31 October 2015

There is no knock on the door. Doesn't happen like that for you. It's nothing with the finality of a knock – no punctuation, no full stop, more a sentence, running out of page. For you, it's Morgan's friend Dave and his girlfriend Stevie, standing in the hallway, watching you come down the stairs, then looking at their shoes because you're Morgan's dad, and you're wrapped in a towel, still wet, still dripping, not fearing the worst, not yet. This is how it happens for you.

'Morgan has been taken to hospital,' they say.

'What's he done this time?' you say.

Six months ago, Morgan slipped on a wet dance floor and broke his ankle. That's why you ask. He is twenty years old. Just getting started. There are a few more bones to break yet.

Did you tell him to take care when you dropped him at the pub this afternoon? You can't remember. You remember him coming into the dining room and asking you for a lift. You remember saying no, because you gave him a lift last Wednesday and he didn't say thanks. You remember Sue telling you to stop being a miserable bugger. And you remember reluctantly agreeing, like you always did in the end, one way or another. You remember him telling you about a job he'd

7

applied for, and that he only realised autocorrect changed some crucial wording on the application the moment he pressed send. You remember laughing together, laughing so much you could barely see the road. You remember him telling you about a new girl he'd started seeing. Maybe he will see her tonight. Life is good. You remember him getting a phone call, so he was smiling and talking to someone when he got out of the car, looking back at you but forgetting to say goodbye.

'We don't know how bad he is,' Dave says, pacing the lounge so much you wonder if he's forgotten how to sit down. 'But Craig who was out with him kept calling, and we thought he was drunk so we ignored his calls. But eventually we gave in and answered, and he said we should come and get you, that it's important. He's in Coventry University Hospital. We don't know how bad he is.'

Sue rings A&E. It's not your local. The nearest one is at George Eliot Hospital in Nuneaton, where Morgan works, just up the road, a ten-minute drive. Anytime there has been an accident, that's where you've gone.

'Has a Morgan Hehir been brought in?' Sue says.

The woman on the phone can't say for sure, but thinks you should just come down. You ask Dave if he can give you a lift. Can't be drinking and driving. You're a truck driver for a supermarket, you'd lose your job. And you've had two beers with a Vietnamese meal, a big bowl of spicy vegetables and meat in liquid you'd call soup, because until a few minutes ago this was just a normal Saturday night.

In a way it still feels like one. Maybe that's why you make light of the situation the whole way there. You talk about his broken ankle. The dance he must have been doing. How it would be just like Morgan to have hurt himself trying to do that very same dance on the very same dance floor, because

8

he never learns, that boy, does he? He just wants to have a good time. To be with his friends. That's who he is. You don't think too much into it really. Your hair is still drying and you're kind of relaxed. How else are you meant to be?

You and Sue enter the hospital through the big automatic doors and you look at each other like, bloody hell, because it's chaos, always is on a weekend, what with all the drunks and idiots.

'Is Morgan Hehir here?' you say to the woman on reception, and you're not even sure if she responds, it's more as though she makes it happen with her mind, because two police officers appear and escort you to a room. A room behind the scenes, where people like you don't go. It's confusing to be here, with a police officer telling you Morgan has been stabbed, and that his condition is unknown. It's confusing when a doctor comes and kneels before your seat like it's a throne and you're a king or something and tells you Morgan has been stabbed in the chest, and it is not good, and he is very ill, but they are doing everything they can. And it's confusing when another doctor comes and tells you he is an air-ambulance doctor who treated Morgan at the scene.

'What . . . in a helicopter?' you say.

'No,' he says, 'we don't fly at night.'

And you briefly feel silly. Of course the air ambulance doesn't fly at night. But you only feel silly for a few seconds. That becomes something you don't really feel any more. Not after this.

'I was on the scene within a few minutes,' the doctor says, gesturing with hands that held your son. And you're thankful, because they look big, they look safe. 'I got his heart going. But he is very poorly. And he has a very big uphill struggle.' You nod and thank him, but your head is not there.

9

Someone asks if you want tea, and you say yes, but you don't feel you've got a body to pour it into. You will put it in your mouth and it will end up on the floor.

You don't know why, but you ask a police officer if it would be possible to bring your other two sons to the hospital. He arranges to gather your family, like sticks. They send a car, and you call Connor, your eldest, to warn him. You tell him Morgan is poorly, and when he arrives he says that's how he knew it was bad. Because you used the word poorly. What kind of word is that for a hospital to use? He arrives with Eamon, who is only fourteen and looks scared, and the four of you hold each other.

You've never been in a hospital at night before. The corridors are empty, and the floors bend the light the way waiting bends the hours. When you look out of the door, you don't know where you are. There are no people and no signs. Not to where you need to be.

A nurse comes. He tells you they are just getting Morgan's blood levels right. You don't know what this means but it sounds good. And you will be able to go and see him soon, so it must be good. He leaves and you drink more tea, an unreasonable amount of tea, until he comes back and takes you all to another room. It's closer to Intensive Care. Closer to Morgan. He's probably only a few metres from here, that's what you think. Behind a door. Behind a wall. You can get to him as soon as they're done patching him up. You'll run in there and hold him in your arms.

In the corner is a vending machine, buzzing like a trapped insect. Beside that is a noticeboard, which you stand and read and read again because you can't think what to say to your children, who are over on the other side of the room with Sue, all of them staring at nothing because they're like you – they can see their worst fears in the empty spaces, they can hear them in the silence. Dread is swelling up inside you, inflating in your throat like a balloon.

On the noticeboard you see it lists the nurses on duty: Carol, Marie and Joyce. It's an omen. Has to be. Sue's two sisters are named Carol and Marie, and her maiden name was Joyce. Sue has spotted it too, you can tell, because she smiles at you nervously, from the corner of her mouth.

You're not really religious, not any more. Though once a Catholic, always a Catholic – that's what they say, isn't it? And you're desperate. So, without moving your hands, without moving your lips, without anyone knowing, you do Our Fathers. You do Hail Marys. Maybe twenty of each, wondering, all the time, if that's enough. How many will it take to help now? What does this cost in prayer?

It's been quiet for so long that it's a surprise when the door swings open. You actually jump a little. You spill hot tea on your fingers, but you don't feel it. A nurse enters.

'We're going to get him ready for you to see him,' she says, and everything feels all right then. 'Have you ever been in Intensive Care before?'

Everybody shakes their heads.

'Don't worry. There will be lots of machines, which can be scary, but there's no need to be frightened of anything.'

The nurse leaves again. Nobody says a word and nobody moves, but the air seems sweeter when you swallow it. You wait again, taking as much of it down as you can.

The last time you took Morgan home from hospital, after he broke his ankle, he had a couple of pins through his leg – a few screws and a metal bracket. You picked him up when they discharged him, and it took forever to get him in and out of the car. You helped him through the door and on to the sofa, and the days and weeks began to pile up. Staying in was torture – for him, because he loved to go out and be with his friends, and for you, because whenever you got comfortable in front of the TV, he asked for a cup of tea, or a sandwich, or help swinging his ankle off the floor. There you were, like a bloody butler, like bloody Lurch, at his beck and call. Up and down so much your back ached. But you had time together. Good, solid time. The kind of time you don't normally get.

After a while there wasn't anything you didn't talk about – his graffiti, his music, his friends – there wasn't anything you didn't know about his life. And though you never once said so, it felt wonderful. These things worry you, as a father. You have an older son, so you know how it goes. It's around now they cut the rope and cast you adrift. They're too old to need you and too young to know how much you need them. You yearn for a past you still see in their eyes. But you were glad to be needed, for a little while longer at least.

Some days you drove him to his hospital appointments, and he would insist you visit the maternity department, where he was a ward clerk. Not delivering babies. Signing them in. It was nice to see how much they liked him at work, all the ladies laughing with him, laughing at him for having time off even though he was carrying more metal than RoboCop. He came home and said to his mum, 'I never knew older women could be so funny.' He was smiling, his cheeks the blush of red apples, always.

Two doctors come in theatre gowns. They close the door behind them and sit down in the chairs opposite.

'I'm sorry,' they say, 'we tried everything.'

That's how you find out your son is dead.

All that love for him inside you, that love with nowhere to go.

You hold each other. The sound Sue makes is unearthly.

'Did he suffer?' someone asks. It might have been you.

'No,' one of the doctors says. And then they leave. There are just the four of you now, for a while, forever.

A nurse says you can see Morgan soon. And you tell that to the man with the face that seems older than the fifty-something he must be who introduces himself as a detective and says he'll take you home. You look down at his feet, because you can't look up and see that beneath his suit he is wearing sports socks. No, you say. You're not going home. They are getting Morgan ready, so that you can see him.

'No,' the detective says, 'you are not going to see him. He is a crime scene now.'

Oh Colin. Here's something you can't know, but maybe you should. Tomorrow, and even years from now, you will not be able to remember this man's name. The pain you feel in this moment will purge it from your memory. You will never remember it, even though you will never forget him.

It's important you know you survive this.

'We're going to see him,' you say, 'when the nurse has got him ready.' That's what she said. You heard her.

The detective shakes his head.

'If you insist, I will have to arrest you,' he says.

You stare at him a while. Like he's joking. But he's not. Who'd joke about this? And no one intervenes. So you, well, you have to agree, don't you? He's a policeman, a detective. And you? You're not you any more.

So, OK then. All right. You won't see your son. Your son who is dead.

Connor and Eamon are taken home by uniformed police, and the detective takes you and Sue out of the Intensive Care Unit, to a set of steps. And you follow him because you need to follow someone, but then he stops and turns round. And then he walks the other way again. And you're still following him. You round a corner, then another, and soon you are back where you began. And you are lost then, walking along corridors, through doors, into rooms without exits, past windows you can't see out of.

When you finally get outside it is getting lighter and there is fog. You emerge from it at your house, half an hour behind your two sons. They are waiting in the kitchen. You exchange a few words and then they go to bed. It is five or six in the morning.

Losing a child has crossed your mind. It crosses the mind of every parent. Flies in like a bat, flaps around until you chase it out because you daren't let it find a place to hang. That's what having a child is, a stretching of the ways it's possible to feel. A new kind of love, a new kind of pain. Previously unopened rooms in the soul. You can't open one door without the risk of opening the other. That's the entry price of parenthood, the unfathomable gamble you make.

But you've never thought about what it really means. What it is to lose someone you love so much so suddenly. What it does to you. How it changes you. What else is taken too. And now? Now you remember when someone tried to tell you.

Her name was Mary. She worked with you, at the chip shop you ran up the road in Bulkington when you were twenty-one. She told you her story, but you were a young man then. Too young to run a business, that's for sure. You were all in your own head, not really listening, just doing your thing. You didn't understand because you couldn't. But now you think about what she was trying to tell you when she told you about her sister, Pauline Swingler, and what happened when the clock struck twelve. Mary was trying to tell you how it put her heart beyond repair.

Now when you think of Mary's story, you understand completely.

A TRAGEDY IN NUNEATON: PART ONE
THE DEATH OF PAULINE SWINGLER

Pauline Swingler was excited. If there was ever a night to put on her best dress, do her make-up and get her hair looking just right, this was it. She was sixteen years old, which in 1965 was the cliff edge of adulthood, and tonight she was going to find out for herself what her future had to offer, because she'd got her hands on the hottest ticket in Nuneaton. The New Year's Eve Dance at the Co-op Hall.

The Co-op Hall was a shabbily resplendent art deco building, and if you were young in Nuneaton in the early 1960s, it was without question the place to be. It had opened in 1939 as a dance hall on the site of a former Co-operative store, and in the decade and a half after the Second World War had become the kind of place where big bands played, demobbed soldiers soberly courted their future wives, and romance was a decidedly formal endeavour.

But by 1965 the town and the attitudes of its people were changing. The last local coal mine was three years from closing, the job market was mutating, a boom in the building of low-cost council housing saw the map expand in every direction, and there was enough of a rise in population – many of them young – that the authorities had no choice but to invest. Much of the town centre was being redeveloped, finally papering over the cracks of bomb damage it had sustained during the war. They were regenerating Nuneaton with the best of 1960s town planning: an indoor shopping centre, a library and a ring road, the town centre's bruised lip.

This is where the Co-op Hall sat. Unable to escape the wave of the new, it reinvented itself as a hip live-music venue, catering for and capitalising on Nuneaton's swelling ranks of youth, all keen to indulge in the cultural revolution, dance and, if things went their way, be kissed in ways their parents barely dared dream about. Because of the Co-op Hall, this little town, slap bang in the centre of England, and lacking the sense of identity enjoyed by the North and the South – a town you'd go through because you had to, sometimes literally had to, just to get up and down the country to somewhere better – had become an unlikely stop-off for up-and-coming touring bands en route to bigger things.

The Beatles played the Co-op Hall on 5 October 1962. They were second on the bill ('For the first time in Nuneaton, fabulous new recording group The Beatles') behind Buddy Britten and the Regents, a proto-tribute act to Buddy Holly and the Crickets, right down to the accent and thick-rim glasses. Second on the bill, but on top of the world. That morning they'd released their debut single, 'Love Me Do'. A year later the hall welcomed The Rolling Stones, who played two shows on 15 November 1963. The first was an afternoon performance for children, where an audience of six- to ten-year-olds pelted the band with cream cakes.

On New Year's Eve 1965, by which time The Beatles and The Rolling Stones were the two biggest bands in the world, Pauline Swingler was too excited to feel the cold as she joined the queue outside the venue. More than 900 young men and women were there that night, so the line stretched way beyond the canopies that protruded from the side of the venue to protect the partygoers from the elements. Nobody seemed to care. Everybody wanted to see Pinkerton's Assorted Colours, a local Warwickshire band riding high on the top-ten success of their debut single 'Mirror, Mirror'.

That fevered anticipation only grew once Pauline finally made it inside the building. She'd never seen so many people in one place, smiling, dancing and holding hands. If this was a glimpse of what her future in Nuneaton looked like, then she couldn't wait for it to arrive.

And arriving it was. There were just minutes to midnight when the DJ in the packed upstairs bar announced that the headline act would shortly be taking to the stage downstairs for their special New Year performance. Everybody rushed towards the one tight staircase, eager to be at the front when the clock struck twelve and the band appeared to rapturous applause.

It was on the stairs that linked the floors like a cramped little warren that one of the first revellers fell. The sheer volume of people behind them and the speed at which they were moving made it impossible for them to stand up again. And so somebody else fell. And somebody else. Soon it seemed everybody was falling, falling until there was no more space to fall into. There were legs and bodies everywhere, getting heavier and heavier until, at the bottom, there was no room left for life.

It took a long time to clear the crush and tend to the seriously injured. When the dead were counted, there were four. Pauline Swingler was among them. Midnight had come and gone.

The Co-op Hall, despite great effort and refurbishment, never quite managed to escape the tragedy and assume its former glory. In many ways its fate seemed to reflect the fortunes of the town. It became a Kwik Save supermarket for the 1980s family on a budget, and, for a while in the 1990s, a Laser Quest, where frantic children could shoot each other with pretend guns. Eventually, having fallen into a state of some disrepair, it was demolished in November 2008.

A sign stands there now, in memoriam to Pauline Swingler and those other poor souls – nineteen-year-old David Greenway, twenty-two-year-old Joseph Brian Peare and fifteen-year-old Keith Harding – whose lives were lost on that terrible New Year's Eve in 1965.

In the cold, dark first days of November 2015, that memorial was surrounded by bouquets of flowers, each with a handwritten card nestled among the petals. They'd been left there by shocked, saddened locals on hearing the news that a young local man, Morgan Hehir, had been murdered just a few short steps away.

Sunday, 1 November 2015

Today you will do the most brutal thing you've ever done to someone you love.

First, you sleep for an hour, maybe less. You're crying when you go to sleep, and you're crying when you wake up. You have things to do but you don't want to do them. How are you meant to tell people what has happened to Morgan? You can't just get on the phone, start calling family members and have that conversation over and over and over again. So you call Geraldine, your eldest sister, at 7 a.m. on a quiet Sunday morning when the sky is not yet newborn pink. She answers sleepily. There is a moment in between the before and after, when a match is struck but not yet aflame. You hear it now. The peace in her voice you're about to take away.

'I'm sorry about this,' you say, about waking her, about everything, 'but Morgan was murdered last night.' It hits you that this is all you know. Not who did it. Not why. All you know is this: someone pushed a knife into him, and now he is gone.

'I'm so sorry, but I can't tell everyone the news,' you say to Geraldine. 'You're going to have to do it. Even Mum and Dad. I just can't tell them.'

You make a noise that will live inside both of you now.

The doorbell chimes. You answer to a rather large man and a woman in normal clothes. Her name is Sharon and she is a police officer. She takes a back seat for all the talking. But the man, he likes to talk. He shows you a badge and they come into the lounge, where he introduces himself as Alan, your Family Liaison Officer, your FLO. The bridge between you and the police. If you have any questions, you will go through Alan. If the police want to know anything, they will go through Alan too. He's a big part of your life now, even though he just walked in, without ever asking if he should take off his shoes.

He needs to tell you something. He sits you and Sue down and says that though it's too soon to know exactly what happened last night, they have arrested someone for the murder of your son. Three people, in fact. They can't say who, or how, or where, because these are the early stages of a live, fast-moving investigation, but there are people in custody. Then he waits. Are you supposed to say something? Shake his hand? Punch the air? Are you meant to feel anything like the gratitude or relief he seems to want that doesn't come? Are you meant to feel anything at all?

You half expect him to present you with a manual. There must be instructions for the grieving parents of murdered children, because behind closed doors up and down the country, this happens to ordinary people all the time. The strange thing is, there must be some kind of mistake, because now it's happening to you.

You stand up and start making tea and coffee, playing host on autopilot for visitors you never wanted. They politely accept, and while they drink the tea you made, they ask all about your families. Your brothers, your sisters, where everyone lives. They go through your entire family tree. A hundred questions that couldn't seem less important when you've just lost your son. But you and Sue are nice, polite, compliant people. You're kind, everyday Nuneaton people. You've never been in trouble, and you make none for no one. So you answer them, because they're police, and they're here to help you, and that's what good people do. You answer every question until they stop, and you wonder if they now know more about you than they do about the men they arrested that morning for killing your son.

Alan says you should keep the blinds drawn. The press are in the area. They may be looking for you. If you speak to the press you could jeopardise the whole investigation. Forty-seven years old, and now you are scared of opening your own front door.

Later, when Alan is gone, there is another knock. And you do open the door. You peek out through the curtain and see it's Joe, Craig and Adam, and you let them in, and make them tea. They look tired. You've met Joe and Craig once before. They're Morgan's drinking and football friends, older than Morgan by seven or eight years. They've come to tell you how your son was killed, because they were there when it happened.

They were walking. Joe, Craig, Adam, Danny, Shawn and Morgan. Nice lads, good lads. A real laugh. It was Halloween, so Craig was dressed as Marcel Marceau – white face paint, braces, stripy shirt, that sort of thing – and Morgan as a priest, with a robe that swished and swooshed a little, head to toe in black. It's half a mile or so from the Town Talk pub to The Crew, a rock bar, and the quickest route on foot is through Nuneaton Recreation Ground. Everybody calls it Pool Bank Street Rec, because it's at the end of Pool Bank Street, which unfurls from the park like a tongue to lick the edge of the town centre. This is the hinterland without purpose between the businesses and shops, and the sprawling estates that haven't yet properly begun. There are unlit rows of garages and squat housing blocks where the rooms are small and cheap. A place where people get put, like the cupboard in the kitchen where the odds and sods are kept.

And then there is this park, with an unloved slide and a swing, its chains always wrapped tight round its crossbar, as though strangling itself but never quite finding the strength to finish the job. There is a thin path through the grass, and if the sun is hot enough workers might eat their lunch here, a quick sandwich, a meal deal, more to escape the office than to take in the view.

On the left-hand side is a block of flats. As Morgan and his friends passed by, around 9 p.m., a group of people were drinking on a balcony. It was a horrible evening, wet and blustery and too dark to make out how many there were, but the music they were playing was loud. One of the men looked down and saw them, perhaps saw Morgan's priest robe, which in the dark that night looked kind of like a hijab, and he shouted:

'Paki!'

It might have been the same man, maybe someone else, shouting:

'Paki!' and 'Paki scum!' and 'black bastards!'

It might have been one of them. It might have been all of them. Who knows how many there were. It took a few seconds for Morgan and his friends to realise it was them who were being shouted at, and where the voice was coming from.

'We're white, mate!' Danny shouted back. 'Fuck off!' And then they walked on.

They were almost out of the park, at the top of Pool Bank Street, in sight of The Crew, when they heard people running towards them. The footsteps were fast and hard like rage.

Adam turned, looked, and only had time to say, 'We're gonna be attacked', before the man in the baseball cap with the can of beer punched him hard in the face, and was joined by another man, maybe two, beating him to the floor, where he lay in a foetal position, the men kicking him in the head and body with a force it's almost impossible to imagine applying to something living. The force you'd end something with. Everything they had.

But Adam was tough. He'd been in the army. He'd been to Afghanistan. He could handle himself. When it seemed his attackers had moved on to someone else – it was hard to tell, everyone had scattered in different directions the moment this began – he clambered to his feet and tried to put some distance between himself and the chaos so he could see if anybody needed help. It was only then, as hot blood poured down his leg, that he realised he had been stabbed in the buttock. He found Shawn not far away and told him to compress his wound – he knew about this because he learned first aid in the forces – and to call an ambulance. Looking back over Adam's shoulder towards the park where it was too dark to really see anything, Shawn took out his phone and dialled 999 while Adam lay on the ground.

Joe had run in a different direction, but he saw Adam get beaten by the men. Maybe there were six of them in total, maybe less, he wasn't sure, a fury of arms and legs. It was all so fast, so frenzied. They caught Craig too, swinging him round by his mime-artist braces, ripping them off his chest and beating him. Joe escaped and caught his breath, or tried to.

When he returned, the fight was over, the men had vanished, and Morgan was lying on his back in the road, twenty or thirty yards away from where the attack began. There was another man there, someone Joe hadn't seen before, a stranger, helping Morgan. While Joe put Morgan in the recovery position – he saw no blood, just Morgan's eyes rolling back – the stranger handed him Morgan's driving licence. Joe was talking to Morgan, telling him:

'It'll be OK, hang on in there mate, wait for the ambulance it'll all be OK, it'll all be OK, it'll all be OK, just hang on.'

It was another minute or so before he realised the stranger had gone, and that he had taken Morgan's wallet and iPhone. He had stolen them while Morgan lay dying on the ground.

It wasn't long before blue lights lit up the dirty walls of Pool Bank Street, and a kind air-ambulance doctor jumped out of a rapid-response car to restart Morgan's heart, there on the road, with his big, safe hands.

Morgan's friends leave and you and Sue sit in silence, all this new information on top of you, not soaking in, like a puddle on the soil of an over-watered plant.

But there is never silence long enough to begin to understand it, because Alan keeps coming back. Three times that afternoon. Four times maybe. He's in and out so much he should have his own key. He likes to talk, does Alan. There are lots of updates in a murder investigation like this, he says, and it's his job to keep you updated. Like about the text message. There is a text message, doing the rounds like the flu, up the road and down the street and around the town. It names the killers. Can you believe that? People click on it, open it up, and there are photographs of them. Three of them. The three men everyone in town is saying killed an unnamed victim last night. You don't get this message. Thank God you don't get it.

But Adam does. One day, not yet, but in the future, when he thinks you're able to hear it, Adam will tell you that he got the text message the very next day after Morgan's murder while he was tending the knife wound in his buttock, wincing, still crying a bit as he pulled up his trousers, so exhausted from the night before he could barely use his hands. He didn't want to know. He didn't want to see their faces because he was trained to remember faces in the army, and he saw them all clearly, recalled them vividly, and one day he might have to do an identity parade. To point and say, that's him, he killed my friend. He chased us and he beat us and he stabbed me and he killed Morgan. Adam wanted to remember what they looked like as they took Morgan away.

But these aren't the photographs Alan has come to talk to you about this afternoon. He needs one of Morgan. A photograph to release to the press. The photograph no parent knows they've taken. And Alan says, choose wisely, because you'll probably hate this photograph soon. It will be everywhere: in papers, on TV, on the internet, and it'll always remind you of this terrible time.

But he's wrong about that. He's so wrong about that. It's not remotely true. Look.

He's so happy. His smile with sun inside. His eyes alight. It's Morgan. Your Morgan. How could you ever hate that picture?

So that's the one you choose. You log into Morgan's Facebook account, and you pick this photograph. And then you, Sue, Connor and Eamon sit in the lounge all evening, crying and copying all of Morgan's photographs on to your own computer one by one and then deleting his account less than twenty-four hours after he died, just like the police said you should in case the press or other people – they never really say who – steal Morgan's pictures. And it feels like you're deleting him. Making him disappear again.

Monday, 2 November 2015

How to talk about normal things? The words come out of your mouth, but they feel cumbersome on your tongue, like moving heavy furniture around. Sue is better at it. No surprise there.

'There are no biscuits in the house,' she says. You're in the kitchen making tea because neither of you can sleep. It's not yet 6 a.m. Doesn't matter, you'll go to the corner shop and buy some biscuits. It opens at 6 a.m. Perfect.

It's damp and horrible, but that's not why you've got your hood up on your coat, the drawstrings pulled tight around your face. It's because you're in disguise. You're paranoid someone will talk to you, that someone will *know*, a paranoia that threads its fingers tight round your sternum, pulling you backwards and diagonally down. But the hood means you can leave the house. Like Michael bloody Jackson or something. Tom bloody Cruise popping to the Spar for a loaf. What must you look like?

It's nice around here. It's the nicer side of town. It's not perfect by any means. But it's nicer, in Nuneaton terms. People living in Camp Hill, or Hill Top, or Stockingford, they'd call this part of town posh. It's not, and neither are you – you don't like posh people as a rule, can't stand anyone up themselves – but it's posh for Nuneaton. It has driveways and detached houses with garages and front gardens and wide roads and well-kept hedgerows and cul-de-sacs. It has caravans and hot tubs and the latest in satellite dishes. If you listen, there are usually kids playing somewhere, riding their bikes on the pavements, OK to be out late.

People round here work hard to live somewhere like this. It's not the kind of place where there's much trouble. It's not the kind of place where anything really happens. In fact, it's a little bit boring. It's definitely not the kind of place where people have a son who gets murdered.

'Good morning,' you say to the woman. She's surprised to see you, but that's probably because she is still unlocking the door of her shop. Her reply is muted, or maybe you're moving away from it fast because you don't want to hear it, and maybe you don't want to hear it in case it's 'Oh, Mr Hehir. I'm so sorry to hear about your . . .'

The newspapers are stacked up. She's not unwrapped them yet. That's good. You grab some milk from the fridge and some biscuits from the aisle and walk towards the till, counting the tiles on the floor like you've already counted the change in your hand, ready to give to her so you can get out of here before anyone else comes. But you're too late.

'What's up with you?' the man says. 'Shit the bed?'

You look up, and through the tight funnel of your hood you see someone you know from work. Another of the HGV drivers. He looks down at the biscuits in your hand. You smile. He smiles back. It's just banter. That's all. The lads at work are giving each other stick all the time, and normally you're as bad as the rest of them. So go along with it. He doesn't know.

He doesn't know.

'Yes,' you say. 'I have. I've shit the bed. You've got me there.' He laughs, and you smile again, like you'll see him in a while, back at work.

Oh fuck. You're supposed to go to work today. You remember – it has still become Monday, somehow. Time hasn't stopped, although it has. What are you meant to do? You can't just ring in and casually tell the person who answers the phone, can you?

'Hello? Yeah, it's Colin. Yeah, I'm all right mate. You all right? Good. Listen. I can't come in today. No, not today. Yeah, yeah. The thing is . . . my son has been murdered.'

So you walk to your boss's house because she lives on the same estate, and at 6.30 a.m. you knock on her door. Her partner answers. He's awake but only just, his eyes still sketches of what they will become. You start to explain, but it's a mess. Only four of the words are words, really.

'My son's been murdered,' you say.

There is a silence. You'll get used to this.

'Oh mate,' he says, his hand on your shoulder but reaching into you, and in that moment he is perfect. You can't say your number because you can't say anything and your hands are shaking, so he takes your mobile phone and finds it.

'She'll text you later,' he says, 'it's sorted.' You want to thank him but you can't.

Holding the family together. That's your job. You want someone to take over and tell you everything is going to be all right, but no one will, so you have to do it and you have to start now. Step up. Come on. Pull yourself together. Isn't that what they say?

OK. All right.

You get home and call Sue's work and Connor's work and let them know. It's easier to help others than it is to help yourself. You'll learn this. You'll learn this a thousand times.

Alan comes again later. You make tea, arrange the new biscuits nicely on one of the good plates, and he asks a few more questions. About Morgan. About the things he was into, the places he visited, the people he hung out with. And because you can't think, because you're in shock, because you still can't believe this has happened, you don't even realise what's going on here, do you? How could you? How could it ever have crossed your mind that you're a suspect? But you are.

Uh-huh. That's right. And though you'll be eliminated from inquiries soon – Alan will tell you so; he'll say you're officially not a suspect in your own son's murder any longer, like you're supposed to be pleased, like you're supposed to wrap your arms round Sue and jump up and down in celebration – it will hurt for the rest of time.

He's still asking questions when a white car pulls up outside. You peek out through the blinds and see it's the driving instructor, here for Morgan's driving lesson. You wouldn't have had to give him lifts much longer, he was doing really bloody well. Same as anything. He was good at stuff, when he put his mind to it. It was just getting him to put his mind to it, that was the thing.

'Shall I have a word for you?' Alan says. You nod, and he goes to tell the driving instructor a little white lie. You don't know what it is but it works. You watch the car slowly pull away from the kerb.

They'll do all this for you, the police, if you want them to. Call work. Tell friends. Lie to driving instructors. They'll investigate whether you had anything to do with your son's murder, and then they'll do all this for you, too. Maybe it's better you do it, though. Do everything while you still can. Tomorrow you'll formally identify Morgan at the morgue, and you don't know if you'll ever be able to do anything else after that.

Tuesday, 3 November 2015

Alan and Sharon arrive early to take you and Sue back to Coventry University Hospital. You are heavy with what you have to do.

He talks all the way. About weather. About football. About this show he watched on TV. Trivial things. At first you don't realise he's trying to help you, but he is. And after a while you talk back. It's uncomfortable, but silence is worse.

This time you don't go through the car park. You're driven round the back of a very large building. Looks more like the back of a warehouse than a hospital, the kind of place bank robbers might meet after a heist in a film. It's private, though. That's why they brought you here. The public can't see in, can't see you push through a set of double doors that seem to sigh as you open them because they've seen faces like yours and know what this means. And you go into the chapel of rest, in the footsteps of parents like you, though it feels they've not been walked before.

A woman greets you. She's dressed like a surgeon, though without the mask. You can see her mouth and her smile, but you can't hear what she's saying. It's as if the words are turned away from your ears because your head is too full.

You sign the forms and Alan asks:

'Is it one of you, or both of you?'

'What?' you say.

'Going in to see him?'

Oh. Well. You hadn't thought about it. But you look at Sue and know the answer immediately. You need her. She needs you. So you are going together.

You leave the reception area, Sharon close to Sue, Alan close to you, uncomfortably close, actually. Maybe you'll faint, maybe you'll collapse, maybe that's why. Maybe he's there to catch you.

'You can't touch him,' the woman says, about your son.

'Why?' you say.

'Because the defendants have the right to a second post-mortem. You don't want to let them claim they didn't get a fair trial and get away with it, do you?'

It's black smoke inside you. That's how it feels. A thick black column of smoke you can't swallow. They have the right to a second post-mortem within twenty-eight days, but you have no right to hold your son? You can't bury him, your boy, until those accused of his murder say it's OK? And you're worried, actually worried you'll touch him, because that's what you've always done. Any time you've seen him, you've reached out and held him, pulled him in close and touched him or ruffled his hair or kissed his face, and actually, now it makes sense, maybe that's why Alan is standing so close. To stop you when you can't stop yourself.

Oh Morgan.

Morgan is lying down. He has a type of shroud around him and only his face is visible. It is very swollen and bloated and badly bruised on one side. He looks almost distorted.

You wish it wasn't him.

But it is.

You both stand staring at him, unable to console him or yourselves.

It's hard to know how long you're there, and when you walk out it's at the angle of people battling through a storm. Reaching the reception room, you're proud of yourself, because you're a man of your word and you promised you wouldn't cry in front of him, that you'd be strong for him. And you were. You walk ten paces along the corridor and then you break down. You cry so hard it moves the air around you.

You ask if you can go back in again, and you do.

No stitch. No pin. No knot. No glue. The rip in you is unmendable.

Alan says his body samples have been taken. His blood. Fluid from his eyes. They removed his brain. They've done more to Morgan than his killers. But you've no choice. It is done. You sign the forms to say it is him. This is Morgan Hehir. This is your son and he is not coming home.

The woman opens the door to let you out, and through tears you say:

'Look after him.'

'I will,' she says. 'I will.'

AN INCOMPLETE LIST OF THINGS THAT HAVE CHANGED

The biscuits last longer.

The bread goes further.

The cornflakes remain in the box.

Fewer arguments about what to watch on TV.

Fewer lifts.

Fewer socks in the basket.

Fewer eyes rolled after bad jokes.

Less money on petrol.

Less laughter.

A fifth less washing flapping on the line.

A door upstairs that doesn't open any more.

Thursday, 5 November 2015

Sue's grief is bigger than she is. It is a bully. It stands up before her and gets in her way, sits down before she does to take her comfy seat. It plays with the food on her plate so she can't eat it and whispers in her ear when she tries to sleep. It waits for her on the threshold of every room to nix what she does next. It is everywhere, thorny and thick. It is muscular. It is whole.

The police are worried she won't be able to handle going to court. You don't tell anyone you might not be able to handle it either, but it's true. You might not. And though it seems impossible to leave her, though it seems like cruelty, like torture, you do it for the same reason you do everything now. Because it has to be done.

So you shower, you shave, you put on a crisp white shirt (your best, usually saved for weddings and funerals). You button it up to the neck, knot your tie the size of a baby's fist and shine your shoes until they look brand-new.

Alan arrives at 8 a.m. and he's surprised. He expected a suit, but not a three-piece. But you want to give the right impression. You want the men they're saying killed Morgan five days ago to see you, and you want them to know exactly who you are.

It's a forty-minute drive to Warwick Combined Court, and you arrive early. Here's a thing. You only go through back doors now. Like a VIP or something. Straight through to the witness-protection part of the court, so you don't have to sit with the public. Means no one can see you. You're relieved about that.

A volunteer shows you round.

'Here is where the judge sits and over there in the bullet-proof box is where the defendants sit.'

It looks exactly like it does in dramas on TV, which is as much as you know about this kind of thing.

'This is where the jury sit and here is where you will sit, which is about three feet from the defendants . . . Is that OK?'

Yes. It's OK. Because it means you will see them at last. You will see the three men charged with Morgan's murder: Declan Gray, his brother Karlton Gray and Simon Rowbotham. Years from now, when people ask you what this felt like, you will tell them you felt nothing.

The wait in the witness room goes on and on and on. There's probably a thing about too much tea being bad for you, and you could find out here if you put your mind to it. You just keep pouring it in, like it's cement that won't set and there's a hole in you to fill.

Eventually a man comes. He says his name is Jason Downes and introduces himself as the detective leading the investigation. He's nice. Respectful. Nervous to meet you. But there is a problem, he says. It's been deemed unfair for the defendants that you are sitting too close to the judge. They're concerned it might be showing a bias towards you. They want a fair trial, after all.

But.

Wait a minute.

You're too lost in grief to tell him what you're really thinking.

Fuck the defendants, they're the ones charged with murder. Why am I the one having to make concessions when they—

So you sit in the public gallery, which is high up on a balcony with a glass front looking down on the court, and you sit with the public after all. You're exactly where you didn't

34

want to be, craning your neck from the cheap seats, because the balcony is right over the defendants' booth, meaning the only way to see them, to really see these men accused of killing your son, is to watch them on a dodgy twelve-inch TV screen through a low-resolution camera which is positioned on them at an angle. No matter how you stretch or squint, you can't look into their eyes. You're denied that, just as you're denied them seeing you. But they know you're there, don't they? Right above them. They must. They must feel you, the heat of you, burning through the floor above their heads, even though you are so cold.

It's over in minutes. The court hears the charges, the defendants confirm their names, and the date is set for a trial: 19 May 2016. Your twenty-sixth wedding anniversary. The day before Morgan would have turned twenty-one. No one asked you, did they? But that's irrelevant now.

All you want is justice.

When you get home you take Sue for a walk across the fields and tell her about the court. You tell her you saw the men they say killed your son and there was nothing human in their eyes. It is dark out. No one can see you, smudged into silhouettes of hedgerows. It is how you need it to be.

TREACLE TOWN

In Saturday morning's fledgling hours, teenagers on their way home from the local nightclub detour through Nuneaton town centre to uphold another dubious tradition steeped more in intoxication than a sense of civic pride. Clambering on to the stone plinth in the middle of Newdegate Square, they plant a kiss on the cold stone lips of the statue of George

Eliot, which is pensively posed, as though in thought or mourning, or perhaps she's just annoyed.

George Eliot was born in Nuneaton – although in more auspicious surroundings than her kissers – on the sprawling Arbury estate. She spent much of her childhood living in Griff House, halfway between Nuneaton and Bedworth, which is now a Beefeater restaurant ('*discover the famous flavour of freshly prepared food, char-grilled to perfection*'). Her first published work, *Scenes of Clerical Life*, takes place in and around the fictional town of Milby, based on Nuneaton. It is full of detailed, realistic depictions of the area's poverty, issues with alcohol abuse, sociopolitical problems and the rampant male aggression she observed, here in Treacle Town.

Nobody agrees why they call Nuneaton Treacle Town. Some say it's because no one ever leaves. That they're stuck, as though in treacle. Some say it's because people in Nuneaton talk slowly, as though words wade through treacle to exit their mouths. Such is local rivalry that three miles up the A444, in Bedworth, they say it's called Treacle Town because the people of Nuneaton are thick.

More likely it's the pace. There's a slowness to life that has characterised Nuneaton since the eighteenth century, when the Birmingham poet William Hutton described the town as being 'in the dominion of sleep'. Walking through it now, past empty commercial units like hollowed ribcages around the lungs of McDonald's and newly sprung vape shops, the pubs that formed the Abbey Run pub crawl whittled down to two, it's hard to argue the town's not in slumber still. But the streets conjure a hard-edged fondness for those who have ever called it home. The people are friendly. The sense of community is genuine. And in the low-slung light of an early spring sun, Nuneaton is as warm as a fond memory.

The mobile butcher over George Eliot's shoulder seems always to have been there, reeling off lists of meat and low prices through a headset microphone without ever stopping for breath. He has outlasted Debenhams, the department store behind him that once felt impossibly luxurious and as though it would last forever. Outside, market traders have always hawked baffling combinations of wares – sun hats and dog toys, strawberries and birthday cards – to an ageing population with an apparently endless desire for such things. Cat ornaments or cakes, flowery dresses or pick 'n' mix; a queue for pastries that never seems to shorten.

But change has brought with it an architectural incongruity. New box flats coax first-time buyers from the tightly packed terraces where their childhood tantrums were heard through thin walls by the neighbours. The glass-walled Ropewalk Shopping Centre wraps around the old Woolworths corpse as though sheltering from a similar fate. There are sleeping bags in doorways, and plucky new café owners trying their luck.

In the days leading up to general elections, TV news reporters appear in Nuneaton town centre, asking shoppers which way they'll vote. Since Tony Blair's landslide New Labour win in 1997 the seat has been seen as an important national bellwether, a key marginal free from the traditional political allegiances of the Tory South and Labour North. In the general election of 2015, it was reported that the moment incumbent prime minister David Cameron knew his Conservative Party had won – and secured a House of Commons majority for the first time since 1992, against the predictions of opinion polls – was when Nuneaton declared for him at 1.53 a.m. But by the time a new prime minister is on their way to see the Queen and the camera crews have all packed up and gone, there is a sense that no one who might change things for the better is watching Nuneaton any more, unless in fleeting glimpses from the window of a speeding train hurtling down the West Coast Main Line.

And so life goes slowly on:

Taxi drivers asking, 'Did you hear what happened Saturday night?'

Neighbours saying in hushed tones over garden fences, 'On Pool Bank Street, by the Rec bab, downtown.'

Whispering in pubs across half-full glasses, 'A knife, love, apparently. Didn't even know each other.'

In the shop buying milk, 'It's tragic isn't it? So sad. His poor family.'

Late at night, in bed, to each other before they fall asleep, 'Only twenty. So, you know. An adult. But . . . only just.'

And calling their children, who've long moved away but still think of the place now and then, 'How could they do something so wicked?'

If between kisses George Eliot's statue were able to wonder, it might be about how much, if anything, has changed around here after all. Whether Treacle Town's present is little more than a reflection of the past she put on paper, before they sat her likeness on a plinth made out of stone.

Friday, 6 November 2015

There is a knock at the door and you're in the kitchen not moving, peering down the hallway at the figure mottled by the glass because you're scared to answer it. Your own front door! Christ. So Connor goes. He opens it just a little bit, peeks out all suspicious, and you contort to fit inside his shadow.

You know they'll outgrow you, your children. You know that one day, sometime in the future, there will be a tipping point when suddenly – or maybe so gradually that only your own inability to deny it is sudden – you will not be looking after them any longer, and they will be looking after you. But you didn't think it would look like this. You thought you'd be older. You thought they'd be counting your pills into little trays with the days of the week marked on so you don't forget. Carrying your shopping. Helping you in and out of the car. Not that they would end up protecting you, physically, with their bodies, as though they are the father and you are the son. But that's what you need now.

There is a woman at the door. She's polite. Nervous. Sorry to disturb you. She says she's Morgan's boss from the hospital. Connor moves aside, but in a way you're still behind him. She's brought flowers and says she's sorry for your loss. Thank you, you say, suddenly aware of what this must look like to her. You're not in a good way. All pale, with bags beneath your eyes the size of elbows. In that bloody ratty dressing gown. What must she think? You look a real mess. Poor woman. Must have taken some guts to knock on your door today. She's kind, but it's awkward and you're grateful when she leaves fast enough.

The flowers keep coming, though. They come all day, and the only reason you don't disconnect the doorbell is that Sue would tell you you're being a dick. Quite rightly. You don't know much about flowers, but they're lovely, lilies and freesias, white and purple and red, pretty but mournful, and soon there are clusters of them all over the house, the air sweet and sticky in your throat. And around them, condolence cards, a hundred or more, all handwritten:

Sorry for your loss.
You are in our thoughts.
Thinking of you.

You read them all, but it doesn't help. It doesn't help one bit.

When the flowers have wilted and died and rotted right through, you won't have flowers in the house again. There will never be cards on the mantelpiece. You won't mark Valentine's or wedding anniversaries. Birthdays will pass un-celebrated. Your love won't look the same as it used to. There can't be anything that reminds you what it is to feel like this.

Beside Morgan's old school is a church. You go to see the priest there, whose name is Father Simon. You've not seen him before, but let's be honest, you haven't been to Mass in ages. Your knees are better for it, but your soul?

He's a nice man, Father Simon, nice and respectful and a little overwhelmed by your double act, you and Sue, the way that when the pain rises you squeeze each other's hands until it passes. Squeezing and releasing like two sides of a heart. You can't have a funeral yet because those bastards haven't released Morgan's body, but Father Simon asks what you want when the day does come and you start talking and can't stop.

You want Morgan's music played in church, from the band – Fade – in which he played bass with Connor. They were good, you always said it. They had so much potential. Connor is still at it. Morgan only quit because he got fed up with gigging up and down the country most weekends when he could be watching football or having a beer with his mates. Young-man problems. But he loved music. He still wrote and recorded it on his laptop. It was always blaring out

40

somewhere when he was in the house. So you want Morgan's music playing and his graffiti there for all to see.

Morgan told you about his graffiti. He'd shown you pictures on his phone when he broke his ankle – his tag in huge, vibrant, colourful letters on what seemed like every blank wall in the county – and talked about how much he couldn't wait to get back to it when he could walk again. You'd been interested. He was excellent at it. But you were too often confused by the language. Nothing makes you feel old like words you don't understand in the mouth of someone whose arse you used to wipe.

Morgan's tag was GRUT. When he first explained it to you it sounded like he was talking gibberish.

'GRUT?' you said.

'Yes Dad,' he said, his cheeks that special, rosy shade of pink they went when you embarrassed him just by being his father. 'GRUT.'

It didn't mean anything, but that wasn't the point. All that mattered was that it was unique to him. If you travel anywhere in the world and see GRUT painted on a wall, it means Morgan got there first.

'OK,' you said, 'whatever you say, Morgan. Whatever you say.'

Sue squeezes your hand again, but in a different way, more a 'shut up now, you've been talking for ages' kind of way, and Father Simon just listens and says, yes, of course you can have his music playing, of course you can display his graffiti. He's got real empathy, Father Simon. You've a nose for it now. He's sad with you, not for you. He's not like the priests you remember when you were growing up. They liked to give you advice and expected you to follow it. To tell you what to do. Mind you, you haven't been older than a priest before. All of this is new.

The funeral director listens too. You call him later that afternoon – his name is Daniel – and when he answers you say the words you've silently rehearsed.

'My son Morgan has been killed and we need a funeral director, but his body is still at the hospital for an unknown time.' You don't say that what you want more than anything is just to have him back.

Daniel is so polite. A nice, polite local boy.

'We would be honoured to look after your son,' he says. 'But I need to let you know that I am of a similar age and I know a few of Morgan's friends. I don't know if that will be a problem for you?'

You don't know this yet, because you can't, but one day, when you're strong enough – and you will be strong enough – you'll finally sort through Morgan's belongings. Every touch, every smell, every picture will detonate a memory, and after a while you won't be sure how much more of it you can take. But eventually, you'll go through his photographs, thousands of photographs you'd no idea even existed, of nights out, and graffiti, and holidays, and gigs, and good times with mates. And one photograph will stop you in your tracks. Because in this photograph, you'll see Morgan and Daniel standing together, with friends, in a bar, smiling. They knew each other, you see. And maybe Daniel was simply too professional, too kind, too unwilling to upset you to mention it on the day you first spoke to him. And it'll mean the world to you that Morgan, at the last, was cared for by a friend.

The days are short and fast, and sleep comes as moth holes in the night. You can't really cook much. There are lots of parts of you that have fallen away and not returned, and this is one of them. Jesus, you can't even make bacon and eggs. Especially not that.

Bacon and eggs on a Saturday morning is a bit of a tradition in this house. You all sit down for breakfast together as a family and Sue cooks, or you do, and woe betide anyone who over-poaches the eggs. Sue's are the best, but you compete with her for praise. It never really comes but it's always worth trying. You love that. You, Sue and the boys eating bacon and eggs round the table, all of them taking the piss out of your cooking until your plates are stained the colours of a waning sunset. You love all of it. The calligraphy of steam on kitchen windows. The insistent percussion of a gas-hob ignition. The scent of a meal, calling through closed bedroom doors. You love it all so much.

Or, you did. But not now. Now, you go out for food. To Coventry, where no one will know you. A quick meal. A quick drink. Then home. That's when you get a text message from Craig. There is a home game at the Nuneaton Borough ground tomorrow and Morgan's friends want you to go. They have made a banner, a banner for Morgan, and they're going to put it up during the match. You sit on the sofa and you read the message a few times. You really don't want to go, but you don't want to let them down. So you message Craig to tell him you will come tomorrow.

Somehow, you will figure it out. And then you lie in bed and wait for the moths.

Saturday, 7 November 2015

Eamon needs you. He is fourteen and he has lost his brother and you have to be there for him. It's the only reason to get out of bed these days. He is going to a friend's birthday party today, and he can't turn up empty-handed, you won't allow it. But you can't face going into town either. Not on a Saturday morning, not in the week when Morgan's face has been on the front of the local papers. Especially not when the market is there, and you can barely walk ten yards without running into someone you know from the pub, or who you used to work with, someone who seems to know all your business. There's a population of, what, 86,000 people in Nuneaton? And they're all linked somehow, that's how it seems, through friends or neighbours or cousins or marriage. And they all talk to you. They give you the time of day. They know you and have known you for years, and fathers knew fathers and grandfathers knew grandfathers, and on and on, backwards and forever. Because that's what this town is like. A beach with no tide. So little is ever swept away.

What are you meant to say to them? What do they want to hear? The thought of it makes you want to crawl into the dying flowers and hide.

So you go to the Spar and you get the biggest chocolate bar you can find on the shelf, more like a bloody pool table than a chocolate bar, because who doesn't like chocolate? That's what you tell Eamon. Who doesn't like chocolate? You are a dad, after all.

Winning is good, but it's not the thing. If winning was the thing, they'd have torn Nuneaton Borough's Liberty Way stadium down by now. No, the people are the thing. That's what Morgan loved about coming here every other Saturday. A few beers. A bag of chips. Talking shit. Singing songs. Walking out of the ground with his mates, still singing, a bit drunk, Morgan filming it all on his phone as Craig trips and lands in a bush and is stranded there like an upside-down turtle, Morgan and the rest of the lads laughing so much it's like they'll never stop, it's like they'll do themselves a mischief. (This will be your favourite video one day. You will watch it over and over and always think *this is him*.) He had some good times here.

There are still a few minutes until kick-off when you arrive. Sue, Connor and you, squeezing through the turnstiles, filing into the ground. You walk on to the terrace, mainly looking at your feet in fear of anyone recognising you. But there is already someone looking at you. You don't know how you know, you just do. You can feel eyes on you. It's the strangest thing, like gravity inside you. And you look up because even though you're terrified, holding Sue's trembling hand in yours, you're polite more than anything. You don't ignore people.

You see this girl staring and realise you know her. You know her eyes even though there are tears glistening in them like silverfish. And it catches you out because it's Emma. Your niece Emma. Why is she here? She lives in Birmingham. Nuneaton Borough are all right, but they're hardly Brazil. You wouldn't travel that far to see them play, would you? Not if you're not from here. Not unless you were mad. And then you notice that behind Emma is Michelle, your other niece. And behind her, all your nephews, all come to support you.

You walk up and you hug Emma and you hug all of them and you look into their eyes and they're crying and you say:

'No.'

Not on your watch. You say:

'No, it's not going to be sad. It's going to be happy.'

Sure, you want to be strong for Morgan. But it's more than that, isn't it? What's the point in being a crying wreck at a football match? Maybe you're saying it too loud, because when you look around, it's not just your nieces and nephews. It's not just your family and friends. It's everyone. Everyone is looking up at you like you're the team coach or something, listening intently while you speak. And now you're the only one on the whole terrace speaking. Everyone has gone quiet. The two teams are on the pitch in the centre circle with their arms woven round one another, they're all listening to you and . . .

Oh.

Now you see what's happening here. It's a minute's silence for Morgan and you've been chatting shit this whole time.

Yeah, you're embarrassed. You want the ground to open and swallow you up. But you still smile. Because Morgan would have laughed. He'd have laughed all week at that one.

The game begins and there's no sign of Morgan's friends until suddenly about twenty guys come marching out of the bar. They're together. A unit. They march all the way round to the stand behind the away goalkeeper and they unfurl a banner, must be twelve feet long, with a picture of Morgan on it, and they sing these words all game:

There's only one Morgan Hehir.
There's only one Morgan Hehir.
There's only one Morgan Hehir.

And then they're bouncing, into the football chants, the ones he used to chant with his arms round them all:

Give me a D (DEE!). Give me an I (EYE!). Give me an S (ESS!). Give me a C (SEE!). Give me an O (OHHHHHH!). Let's go to the disco, la la la la la.

And it's a riot. It's so funny, the poor away keeper getting barracked, Morgan's face moving with the swell of the crowd like he's in there with them. And he is. And so are you. Smiling and laughing in the middle of this mess.

All the stadium claps at the twenty-minute mark, a minute for every year of his life. The loudest clap you ever heard.

*

Tam and Helen come for a Chinese takeaway in the evening. They're your best friends. They can't possibly know how much of your shit they're going to have to put up with over the next few years (and it's going to be a lot, you're going to drink as much as you cry, and you're going to cry whenever you drink), but you'd do the same for them, you'd do anything for them, and they know it. You put music on, drink wine and cry a lot, and it's not like it was at the football with all that singing and smiling. Now it's miserable. It's always miserable if you peel back the layers and peer inside.

When it's coming up to 9 p.m., one week since it happened, panic slides into you. From nowhere it appears, and it rifles through your thoughts to find the one that hurts you most.

I can't believe he's gone.

You can't think of anything else.

Sue has an idea: 9 p.m., one week on, would be a good time to let off some Chinese lanterns in the garden. Light them, let them float into the sky, to cut through the dark as Morgan did, and remember him.

You light them. Let them go. But the cold evening saps the heat from the air inside and they're barely off the ground before they crash into the bush and set fire to the grass. And you're laughing. A week on, you're all laughing. It should have been poignant, but you almost burnt the shed down. He'd have loved that too.

It's OK to laugh, isn't it? You wonder that. But you don't know. So you stop. You stop laughing and you go inside and you weep and drink too much, because you can't believe he's gone. You just can't believe he's gone.

They're not memories. They're more than that. Memories warp and shift. But these, they're real. They're solid. Like

47

bones. Like flesh. They're parts of you. Extra bits of your body you've grown across time. You like the weight of them. Their heaviness on you. The tracks where you've dragged them through the mud. It's how you measure your life, looking back. The deeper those tracks the better.

His birth was the first. You didn't think you'd be able to love another child when you only had Connor. It felt like there was no other love in the world, that you and Sue were hoarding it all. But you were wrong. Morgan came and he was beautiful and there was more. You were so lucky. He was such a happy little baby.

Morgan idolised Connor from the beginning. He was always chasing him, taking his hand, looking up into his eyes and repeating what he said.

You introduced them to golf. There is no better game for following someone around wishing you could be like them than golf. You were like all dads, you suppose. You hoped one day they'd become sports stars and make all their money doing something they loved, and that you'd get a few free tickets to the Open and your mortgage paid off into the bargain. The only problem was they weren't interested. Especially Morgan. That laugh, though. That laugh when he belted the ball as hard as he could because you'd told him golf was a game of nuance and precision and he knew it'd get on your nerves.

That laugh again, but in Ireland, where you'd go most years, staying in Sue's dad's holiday home with Sue's sister and husband and their family, maybe ten of you in total. Morgan's cousin Grace came in panicking because Morgan had seen that craze about putting Mentos in a bottle of Coca-Cola to make it explode and so he'd decided it would be a good idea to eat all the Mentos and then drink the Coca-Cola. And he was screaming, running around, holding his belly, laughing, saying he was going to explode like a volcano. For a second you worried he might. But his laugh. His laugh. You hear it now when you close your eyes.

Oh God, Morgan.

Another memory: the magic shows he used to do with Connor, with you filming on your camcorder. Morgan making Connor disappear inside a cardboard box. Drumming on the side with his toy wand.

Another one: playing for the local football club and spending all the time he should have been training writing 'GOAL 5' on the T-shirt he wore beneath his kit, so that if he scored five goals he could whip off his top and run towards the crowd of laughing parents spinning it above his head. And he did, the little bugger, of course he did.

Another one: sitting with Eamon, who was just a babby really, and Morgan aged eleven, playing note-perfect renditions of Coldplay songs on the little keyboard in the Early Learning Centre, looking like a giant because the toys are so tiny, grinning from ear to ear, all the other parents thinking how amazing he was. And he was.

Going to big school. Getting a girlfriend, doing as little work as he could get away with, still doing well in his exams. Discovering graffiti, making art, hanging out with skateboarders and artists, the most interesting people, people he loved. Studying at the Academy of Music and Sound in Birmingham, focusing on his bass playing, learning how to make a living from the music industry. Becoming a man. Making records with Connor, pressing vinyl, playing gigs, still looking up to his big brother in exactly the same way he'd done since he was little, and wanting to hold his hand.

All these parts of you, never heavier than now.

SEVEN THINGS YOU LEARN

1) You can't sleep for more than five hours. The first words in your mind on waking, maybe for the rest of your life, will be 'Shit, it's real.'
2) Opening his bedroom door, seeing everything just as he left it, will hurt you every single time.
3) Home-made food tastes fantastic. Sue's brother Mark and his partner Ruth, Morgan's godparents, bring a home-made cottage pie, and when you take a bite you're convinced of divinity.
4) They can't find Morgan's phone and wallet so they're going to appeal to the public for more information.
5) Watching TV is all but impossible. *Murder, She Wrote. Murder on the Orient Express. Midsomer bloody Murders*. The world is full of cruel reminders.
6) You're struggling.
7) Morgan will be laid to rest at the cemetery near the town centre, past the rehearsal rooms where Connor and Morgan's band used to practise. There's a plot there, right by the railway line. Trackside. Graffiti artists love trains. It's going to be noisy. It's going to be perfect for him. You just want to have his funeral. You just want his body back. You just want him with you. There can be nothing else until then.

Tuesday, 10 November 2015

Detective Jason Downes sits on your sofa with Alan, you make them tea, and he tells you that one day – not now, but one day – you will have to watch the CCTV footage of Morgan being killed, because Morgan's murder was captured on camera.

Oh God.

It's good-quality footage, he reckons. Shows the balcony and the boys walking past and how they suddenly ran down and chased them and attacked them. All on the tape. Clear as day.

Detective Downes finishes his tea. He sets his mug down and looks you in the eye. He's not like those other coppers. Not the big shoulders, rugby-playing types. The big, brash types. The hard men. He's slighter. More thoughtful. More quiet. More detective-y. So when he speaks this way, when he leans in and says something, it's important, you can tell. And he says this:

Declan Gray. Twenty-year-old Declan Gray. Who they say had the knife. Who they say put the knife into Morgan. Well, Declan Gray had only been free from prison for four months, because until then he'd been serving a four-and-a-half-year sentence for a manslaughter committed when he was just fifteen.

That's another thing you learn. Declan Gray had killed before.

Thursday, 12 November 2015

Olivia is the victim support counsellor. She sits in the big armchair in the lounge and you all sit around her, hoping she can tell you how to make this stop. She's in her early thirties, so still young, and you've so many questions that your mouth can't form. She, on the other hand, always asks really simple questions. There aren't many people who do that any more, or maybe there are just no simple answers.

'How are you all?'

It isn't that you want to talk so much as you want to be heard. You weren't like this before. You used to be quiet. But now what is on won't switch off. You talk and talk and talk and only stop when your jaw feels like it might drop off your face.

Olivia asks if anyone wants to have a one-to-one session with her, and you all take it in turns to go off into the conservatory for a long chat. Everyone except Sue, that is. She wants the boys to have their turn and says the poor girl must be exhausted from listening to you lot. She says that every time. And that's OK. You're learning how to do this. How to lose a son. How to lose a brother. How to lose a part of you. You figure out early on that you all deal with it differently, you all feel different things at different times. It's OK if you're not all the same. You are divided by the pain that unites you.

Your family come. Your brother David and his wife Maggie, with a beautiful lasagne, her family's recipe. Your sisters, Geraldine and Karen. Your mum and dad. It's like a weird Christmas. Christmas, except absolutely shit on every level. Everyone crams into the lounge and looks at you, as though waiting for a speech. You try to say something, but it's awkward. You're too heavy. Your mouth barely opens. It's such hard work having people around.

Nothing prepares you for seeing your dad cry, though. It sounds stupid, sounds macho. And you don't mean it that way. But to a child, and you are still his child, a crying father is the end of a road.

'Morgan was such a lovely kid,' he says. Your mum tells you he's been crying a lot, and you tell him you've been crying a lot too, and you hug him. His arms are weak around you, his breath shudders softly on your neck. You don't say anything, but you need to get out. So you say excuse me Dad, like there is some urgent business to attend to, and you take the next lot of dying flowers to the recycling bin. There are so many in there you have to get on top and push them all down and it's good because it takes a long time so you're alone for a while. You push them all down until you hear them snap.

There's a vigil in the evening, at the church. Tam and Helen organised it, which was kind, but you can't go. It's too much. There will be too many people, looking at your face, seeing your eyes. Tam understands, you hope. But you get a few messages from friends. People you've worked with at the chip shop or driving a truck. Old faces around town.

All right mate?
Been a while.
How's tricks?
Heard about the thing, with your son.

They ask if you're going to the vigil. If you fancy a pint after. You switch off your phone.

There are 300 people at the church, they say. There to remember Morgan. To try and make sense of what's happened. To pay their respects. There are 300 candles. Maybe it's their warmth you finally fall asleep in.

Sunday, 15 November 2015

All you want is Morgan's body back so that you can lay him to rest, but you have to wait until the police release it, and they won't do that until the accused's defence team say they're happy with the post-mortem and allow it, a declaration they're entitled to a full month to make. So here you are, your anxieties growing with your anger, your sadness deepening with your loss, in a situation where the people who killed your son are preventing you from burying him, and every day they make you wait is another day you're surrounded by reminders of the things he's not here to see. Things like this.

Craig texts to say how much Morgan had been looking forward to this one. And what a day it was. Nuneaton Borough won 5–1 away at Telford. The game was dedicated to Morgan, and his name was lit up on the scoreboard, with his banner hung off the side of the stand. The team even signed a shirt for you. You look on Facebook and see picture after picture of the boys enjoying themselves, getting drunk, tasting victory. There is a video from the train journey back, too, all the boys chanting, 'Let's all bounce for Morgan, let's all bounce for Morgan, la la la la.' It's probably annoying for everyone else travelling. But watching the bystanders, you can see the anger and confusion on their faces slowly fall away as they see the love in the eyes of these young men. Some of them even join in with Jack and Craig, Dave and Joe, until eventually the whole train is bouncing. Bouncing for Morgan. Because there are no rules in this. If you love someone and they're gone, make a banner. Make a stranger hold it high above their heads. Do what you have to do.

That's what you do today. What you have to do.

You're taking out the empty beer bottles, or washing up the wine glasses from the night before, when, out of nowhere, the street where Morgan died pops into your head. Usually when this happens you stop, grip hold of the kitchen counter and wait until it passes. It always does eventually. But today, before you know it, you're driving there. You're moving away from your home, out of your estate, towards the town centre, picking up the ring road, which is busy, and you're amazed by all the people and cars and life being lived. The way things go on.

You're reaching the traffic lights to turn into Pool Bank Street, but suddenly you change your mind. Instead you carry on.

That's all right. Don't worry. Imagine the misery it will cause you. Imagine how mad Sue will be.

But you go down the ring road a little further, see the sign for Lidl, and then turn round. You don't know why, but you turn round, peel off at the lights and park up. Getting out, you can hear music from the bar they never got to. An audience of dying flowers are tied to the railings. And for the first time in a fortnight, you're not afraid. It's dark, it's quiet, you're alone, but you're OK. You put one foot down and then the next and you approach the flowers, reading the little messages from strangers.

What would it look like, to someone passing? A man on his own at night time, trying to read in the darkness. If they asked what you were doing, would you know the answer? To find him? To feel him? To know him again?

No. You'll always know him.

So you stand there and instead you feel nothing. You've no feeling about this place at all. Morgan didn't die here. This place is not him.

You tell Sue what you saw, but it means nothing to her either. She never wants to go, and she's surprised that you did, but she's not angry. Whatever gets you through.

For her it's a tattoo. She's been on Facebook as well. Loads of Morgan's friends are getting tattoos done, with the money it costs them going to the fund Jack and Craig set up. The first you knew about the fund was when you accidentally caught it on the BBC news. You and Sue have been avoiding any media coverage of Morgan's murder as best you can. It's simply too painful to watch. But things people have said – Alan, Morgan's friends, your family at the football – mean you've been aware it's out there, like a wild animal prowling around a place you dare not go. Jack and Craig, they don't know you really, but they wanted to do something for you, to help with the funeral costs. So they set up a JustGiving page and put collection tins in all the pubs and chip shops around Nuneaton. Well, you're not a charity case. You're a proud man. You can borrow the money from the bank to give Morgan the burial he deserves. They should give the money they raise to a real charity.

'Listen,' Sue says. She does that face that makes you listen. 'These people want to help us. You can't give their money away. It's for Morgan.' And you understand then. Let them help. Never forget what this town did for you. There are good people here too.

'I'll get one too,' she says. 'A tattoo.' Not now. One day. You agree. So will you. Have it on you like a medal.

Eamon says he'll get one too.

'You're fourteen,' Sue says. 'So no you bloody won't.'

You both do it, eventually. Even though you both hate tattoos, you do it. On your forearm, a tattoo like the one Morgan once told you he was going to get, with palm trees stretched across the orange of a dipping sun. On Sue's arm, the names Connor, Morgan and Eamon, woven through a vine, wrapped round her always.

Monday, 16 November 2015

There is no real reason for it, not one you can name, but this morning you wake up and for the first time you feel OK. You feel good. The pain is there, of course. But your bones aren't hollow. Your mind is sharp. You're not about to take the entry exam for the Royal Marine Commandos or anything, but you feel all right. Like you can do something. Clean the house a bit. Walk up a hill. And even though you know it's a temporary reprieve, that soon you'll be overcome with anguish again, it's lifted for now and you're thankful. Maybe your grief is as tired as you are.

It's a good job you feel strong because Alan calls, and after you've asked him about getting Morgan's body back (he doesn't know, and you grow so desperate you lose the power of speech for a second), he says he wants to talk about Morgan's iPhone. It's something to do with the theft, but he can't give details yet. He's sorry for making you go in Morgan's room, but he needs the numbers off the iPhone box. Morgan was terrible with mobiles. Could barely hold one without losing it or breaking it. You joked about taping them to his hands sometimes. That he must have had shares in Apple. All these things dads say that don't mean anything, until they do.

You steel yourself before you open the bedroom door, but you do it. You take a deep breath and you search through his stuff (the clothes, hung, still with his shape and shoes waiting to be stepped in). It's not long before you find three boxes. Alan comes with evidence bags to take them all. While he's there you give him Morgan's MacBook too. It's not like his Facebook account. You don't know the password and can't get into it. What if Morgan's iPhone had photos that could be of use to the investigation and what if they were also on his laptop? They're all linked these days. That's how it works, isn't it? The cloud? Morgan used to take care of all your IT stuff for you, just like he did for the ladies at work. It would get on his nerves, you badgering him to explain things, or download things, or make these things make sense, and that amused you no end. There is some pleasure in obsolescence.

Alan can't promise anything. That's what he says.

Mary. Mary at the chip shop, whose sister Pauline died in the tragedy at the Co-op Hall. You've been thinking of her lately. Thinking of what she said, how she got through it. And now you've got this sharpness back, this window of clarity that will close again soon, you remember something else she told you. About a special place she found after Pauline died. Where she went to look for peace and solace, for a gap in the clouds of her grief. Mount St Bernard Abbey, in Charnwood Forest, Leicestershire, where the trees, the sky and the ring of wild rocks form a crown around the vista. A sanctuary for Trappist monks. A place for the troubled.

Now you're here. You and Sue and Eamon. You hold Sue's hand and walk around the grounds, and looking up at the monastery whips the breath from your lungs. Then you go into the small gift shop to find a monk behind the counter, which isn't really what you expected, but everything has to move with the times you suppose. The monks here brew the only Trappist beer in Britain, so, you know, it'd be hard to argue they didn't provide solace for everybody.

Sue and Eamon sift through the religious trinkets and you're just browsing the books when you notice the monk smiling at you. You look down and look back up and it's strange, to have a monk smile at you. His lip is curled like a question mark, as if asking – why are you here? So you do what you wouldn't have done a while ago. You approach and say hello. And you're not even sure he speaks, but out of nowhere you start to tell him what happened to Morgan. You've no idea why, but you do. It spills out of your mouth like you are bleeding it.

You look down at the rosary beads and cross he has placed in your hand. He sprinkles holy water across them and says a prayer. It's so quiet, you can hear everything, can still hear the prayer when it has stopped being said, like it's on repeat until it's answered. It's how they should be, you suppose. He offers his heartfelt sorrow for your loss and asks you to put Morgan's name in the dedication book in the church. This means they will say prayers for Morgan every day, and you like the thought of that. The looping, endless prayer of a monk in a gift shop.

You leave the shop and step into the church. It's peaceful, tranquil. Almost like another world. There's the real world, then yours, then this, and yours and this are closest now. You say a few prayers and sit in silence for a while, the three of you. Then you put Morgan's name in the book and light some candles for him, knowing that, in one way or another, they'll always burn.

As you leave the church there is a station of the cross in the garden, so you go round to look at it, a re-creation of the path of Christ to his death. Eamon has the Polaroid camera and is taking photos, and this makes you feel good. You've encouraged him to use a camera, to be creative like Morgan and Connor became at his age, thinking maybe it would help with his pain. He takes black and white pictures of the building, and there is beauty in them, but an awful, lurking gloom too.

You find Sue alone at the station of the cross. It is under cover, beneath a straw roof, and she is inside looking at Mary with her son being taken down from his crucifixion. You look at Sue and you don't say anything. But you see it and you feel it. You see and feel the pain in her, looking at a mother tending to her dead son before he is buried. The pain of a mother. And you want the solace of this place, centuries' worth, all it has, to rise from the ground around her. To move around her now with arms as solid as those old grey bricks.

Sunday, 22 November 2015

There is no moving forward until you've laid him to rest. No processing what's happened. No returning to work. No way to even ask the questions you need answering if you're ever to have peace again. But they make you wait. So you try to find him in other ways, because, in desperation, in despair, what else is there that can be done? And today you do it. Today you make bacon and eggs. Today you get the eggs perfect.

Afterwards, Sue puts on a DVD of photographs you made a few years ago, back when that was a thing. Pictures of Connor, Morgan and Eamon together. Laughing. Playing. Messing around. Being lads, really. Just being lads. You cry so much, but you feel good about it, even though it's like your heart is rolled through the hot fat in the pan.

You don't dwell on it, though. You think about what Olivia says every time she visits, about how good it would be for you to get out and exercise if you can, and you go to the shed. Wiggling the key in the padlock until the door opens, you're hit with that musty smell air gets, the old-coin tang of dust trapped in cobwebs. You take out your bike and see it has a puncture. The rubber tyre hangs like wet washing. Sod's law, that mate. Typical.

Then you look at Morgan's bike. And it's funny, but somehow you know – more than thought, more than instinct – you should ride it. You should get on it, like you'd never have done when he was here because he'd have made you get straight off again. So you do. You take it out of the shed, wipe it down with your sleeve and go out into the fields behind your house, accelerating down the mud path so fast that birds burst from the hedgerows like bullets.

The saddle waggles around between your thighs. Morgan asked you to fix it ages ago and you never got round to it. How many things are there like that? What else didn't you do? Were there questions you didn't answer? Promises you didn't keep? All these little nicks in time you can't fix now.

What you can do is go forward. You come up off the saddle and drive all your power through your legs. All your energy. All your strength. You imagine your legs as giant pistons, firing as you speed across the fields. Through the scythes of long grass, slicing at your shins. Hitting puddles so quickly you're gone before the mud sticks to your skin. Acid burning in your muscles. You go so fast you wonder if you're invisible. If what you've become is air.

And then you realise. No. You're just a middle-aged man dressed in Lycra on a pushbike. That what you actually look like is bit of a twat. Nice one, Dad. That's what he'd have said, if he could catch his breath for laughing.

A quick turn on to the canal path and you're on the ten-mile circuit where you and Morgan used to time your runs to compete with each other. You notice a leaf on your front wheel, zipping round and round, then the thorn attached to it, piercing through the rubber. Then the pressure dropping, the bike sticking, the air slipping out to abandon you, and as you hit the muddy part of the path the saddle you never fixed spins ninety degrees, the wheel bucks, the frame judders, and you fly up into the air, turning your body at the last minute so you only just avoid landing in the canal, the surface of it slowing with the first rafts of ice, and you're planted on your arse in the mud, laughing like a bloody maniac. Laughing all the way home, carrying the bike Morgan asked you to fix like you carried him enough times. And you're happy. You're bruised, you're tired, but you're happy.

There's a butterfly in the garden when you get there. A butterfly in November. It's sitting on a fence, watching you blast the mud from the bike with a hose, slowly opening and closing its wings, which are brown with big blue eyes. Like it's been graffitied. Like he did it.

You won't see signs one day. They won't appear, or you'll stop recognising them, because you don't need them any more. But for now, this is a sign. Morgan is watching over you. And he's probably wondering what the hell you've done to his bike.

You show Sue the butterfly but she says nothing. She doesn't need to. It's obvious what she thinks. She thinks you're a knob. Sue is always right. And the butterfly flaps its wings a final time, before it chicanes through the sky.

Monday, 23 November 2015

Neither you nor Sue have returned to work yet, and you don't know how or when you will. Your employers have said take all the time you need, which is good, because right now you can't even imagine walking through the doors. How are you meant to function when most days you can barely get dressed? But normality comes. It seeps in. You can't stop it. When the pipe is rusted, the water pushes through.

That's how it is when Eamon comes downstairs in his school uniform. It's so clean, so well pressed the way Sue has ironed it, it feels like a vision from before. He's apprehensive, of course he is. Three weeks is a long time out of school, out of living. But you do your best to reassure him. It will be good for him to be around his friends. They're good kids. He's a good kid.

You and Sue go to the school with him for a meeting to tell them that all you want is for Eamon to settle back in gently. There are mock exams coming up, and Eamon has an eye on them, but you don't care about those, he's been through too much. You just want him to be as happy as he can be.

He'll be OK, won't he?

You and Sue say this to each other a lot. In the kitchen. In the evenings. In bed when you can't sleep. He'll be OK. He's such a strong boy. Much stronger than you were at that age. Maybe stronger than you are now. He's so caring, so gentle. He wants to do well in life. He'll be OK, won't he?

The rhythm of normal life begins again. You can't stop it, even if you don't feel it.

Tuesday, 24 November 2015

There's news. Alan calls, and you're shaking because you want him to tell you they're finally releasing Morgan's body so you can give him a funeral. He says he needs to speak to you in person because he has something big to say. This is it. It must be. It has to be. You drop Eamon off at school, and when you get home Alan arrives and he tells you what it is.

And you're angry. God, you're angry. You're so angry smoke comes up in your throat again, thick and black and hot.

63

Get this. Alan tells you that one of the defence solicitors – and this is just the first part, a bad part, but not even the *really bad* part – one of the defence solicitors is *your* solicitor. Your fucking solicitor. You've used him loads of times. You used him when you bought your business. You used him when you sold it. You used him when you bought your home. How can *your* solicitor be defending one of the men accused of *your* son's murder?

'There must be some conflict of interest, right?' you say to Alan.

'I'm sorry . . .' he says.

'But he knows my family.'

'He might just have been the duty solicitor that night . . .'

'How can he do this? He knows my family.'

You can't forgive this. It's a new feeling, this one. Betrayal. But that's not the worst of it. Alan has more. Brace yourself.

The defence solicitors have made arrangements for Morgan's second post-mortem. They've waited until the last possible day they could under law to sanction it. To put Morgan through that again. To make you wait for his body. To make you wait before you can lay him to rest, and now you must wait at least another week for what you want more than anything else in the world. Him.

You're angrily pacing the lounge, and Alan doesn't know what to do with himself. Whether to sit or stand. How to calm you down.

You head to the Borough ground later, to see the room where the wake will be held when it can finally happen. It's a nice big room, especially when it's empty like now, and it seats up to 200 easy. Dave comes, the chairman. He's charming, a real people person, very helpful, and you discuss the date, and once that's done, almost everything is set. The music.

The photographs. The clothes you'll wear (a trip to town for you, Connor and Eamon, new suits).

Then Dave says something you hadn't thought of before. The wake has to be over by 4 p.m. as he has to consider the safety of the staff.

The safety of the . . .

Oh. Wait a minute.

Morgan was murdered. People were arrested. He's worried Morgan might have been involved with dodgy types. With wrong 'uns. Plenty of those in Nuneaton, after all. He's concerned there might be retaliation or payback or something. And it only occurs to you now that maybe this is what other people are thinking too. So few of your family or friends have asked you exactly what happened that night. They've skirted round the issue instead. And you realise now it's because they're thinking that, for Morgan to have been stabbed to death, he must have been involved in crime, or violence, or drugs, or knives, or gangs. How else does a seemingly ordinary, hard-working, good young man with nice brothers and nice parents find himself in a rough part of town, and in a fight, and being killed, if he wasn't up to something bad himself? People like that don't get murdered. They certainly don't get stabbed to death. Doesn't happen to people like Morgan. Doesn't happen to a good son.

But it happened to yours, didn't it? And you'll never forgive anyone who thinks, even for a second, that he must have had it coming.

'We can flag it with the police,' you say. 'They can be there.' You negotiate with Dave. You understand where he's coming from, but you're good people, honest people, not-any-trouble kind of people. There will be a lot of mourners at the funeral, and it'd be better if you can go on a little bit later. And he says, all right, 5 p.m.

That will work. It's not like it's an Irish funeral. Sue's dad is from Connemara, her mum from Waterford, your mum from Donegal, your dad from Clare. All the funerals back there involve so much drinking, nobody can remember how they end. You just have to hope the priest stays sober. It's more like a party than anything. And maybe all your family are coming over thinking Morgan's funeral will be like that. Fair enough. It's what they're used to. Makes sense in a way, everyone mucking in, everyone bringing food.

But it won't be. Not this time. This won't be a party at all.

Friday, 27 November 2015

In the garden the big tree is bare. Black branches spread, thread veins across the moon. Brittle brown leaves crack like burnt skin. They fall down and you pick them up, just to get out of the house.

Sue is watching from the kitchen window, but you're not sure if she sees you, or if you're part of the blankness. You say come help and she does, the two of you, picking up leaves off the grass.

She isn't there, this woman you love. It takes all her energy to lift them.

You and Sue met at school in Birmingham, in a part of the city where it seemed everyone had Irish parents whose accents confused the locals. You were in the year above her, but you were very different pupils. She was studious, keen. Destined for good marks in her exams and the decent, proper job at BT she waltzed into as soon as school was over. But you weren't interested. Not in the work, anyway. Anything that involved opening up a book and being told what to do by a teacher didn't sit right with you at all.

You were always there though, hanging around the building, bunking off lessons, because you loved being with your friends. This explains three things: firstly, why Morgan was exactly the same (he always hated being on his own, right from when he was a baby). Secondly, why you messed up all your exams and had to repeat a year in sixth form. And thirdly, how you came to meet Sue, when really you should have been gone.

You fancied her immediately, but you were still at an age where it was far easier to learn an instrument, form a band and write some songs that might impress a girl than it was just to tell her straight you thought about her day and night. So that's what you did. You and a friend, you formed a band, Test Configuration. It was the height of the New Romantic era. Music, fashion and sex were changing in ways that confused fathers, especially Irish Catholic ones. At the age of sixteen, you somehow bagged yourself membership of the Rum Runner, the club on Broad Street where, just a few years before, a group of staff (Roger Taylor, the glass collector, Andy Taylor, the cook and maintenance man, John Taylor, the bouncer, Nick Rhodes, the DJ and Simon Le Bon, recommended as a vocalist by an ex-girlfriend who worked there) formed a group and called themselves Duran Duran. It was a scene all right. And you, Colin Hehir, had a card that guaranteed entry. The keys to the bloody kingdom. To a teenager holding a torch for a pretty, studious girl he kept seeing around the place, it was worth its weight in gold.

'How do you fancy coming to the Rum Runner?' you said.

'I've always wanted to go there but it's impossible to get in,' she said.

You hid your smile. You played it cool.

'I'm a member,' you said. 'And I'm in a band.'

That first date went well enough: even though your best mate threw up over her friend, even though Sue says she knew from the off you were a Brummie bullshitter, you got a second date out of it. Maybe it was on that second date you figured out both your parents got married on the very same day as each other, decades before – the kind of coincidence that might convince a couple of kids who still believed in God that their story was written in the stars.

There's a photograph of you, taken on the night of that second date, a little over six years before you got married yourselves, in 1990, aged just twenty-three and twenty-two. A photograph taken before everything, really. Before so much loving was done. Before your lives were made together, before your lives were wonderful, before your lives unspooled.

Tuesday, 1 December 2015

The traffic on the school run is horrendous. You get Eamon there in time, just, but the way home is even worse. Traffic is a part of your job. You've a kind of affinity with it, a truck driver's sixth sense for when to risk a detour, or when to stick with it and hope for the best. But you don't need to be a trucker to see this is totally buggered, so you nip down past town, over the Cock and Bear Bridge, off the roundabout at Queens Road, which runs all the way down to Pool Bank Street like a fault line through your pain.

As you get closer to Lidl at the bottom of Pool Bank Street, you notice eight or nine police officers lifting up a manhole cover. There is no one else in the world who could look at that and think, yeah, that's something to do with us. But you can, and you do. And you're right.

An hour or so later, when you're finally back home and you've got your feet up and you're flicking through the channels looking for something, anything, that might distract you for five minutes, Alan comes. He explains they've arrested someone for the theft of Morgan's wallet and phone, even though they still haven't been found. And you don't know what to say. There is nothing you can say.

Afterwards you go into Morgan's bedroom. The grief is like a vice there, clamping you to his bed and crushing you, but also, right now, the only thing holding you together.

Wednesday, 2 December 2015

People are good, you know. Fourteen thousand pounds. That's what they raised for you, those boys. How many people in this town must have put their hands in their pockets for that? Goodness is everywhere if you open your eyes to it. When you go to put the bin out you see, across the street, the lady who delivers the free newspaper, her heavy, print-scuffed fluorescent orange bag flung across her shoulder. You've seen her loads of times, but never really spoken to her before. Just nodded, waved maybe. But today she crosses the road, and before she even gets to the lip of the driveway there are tears in slalom down her face. She throws her arms round you, holds you tight, and tells you she hasn't dropped a newspaper through your letterbox since Morgan died because the papers were full of your story. She knew who you were and didn't want to upset you. That's kindness, isn't it? You smile, which relieves her a little, and you ask if you can start having

69

papers again now. She nods, laughs, rolls one up and presses it into your hand.

Friday, 4 December 2015

The police finally release Morgan's body and the relief you feel is immediate. You, Sue and Connor arrive at the funeral director's to see him. Now you can plan the funeral properly. Now you can start to say goodbye.

Daniel welcomes you. You are focused on what it is you have to do. He calmly asks if you're ready, and then – it's not slow-motion, but it's not real-time – you follow him along a corridor, to the Catholic room. Daniel explains this is where Morgan is, behind those doors, candlelit beneath a statue of the Virgin Mary. When the doors open, you smell the sweetness of his aftershave.

Morgan is lying in a coffin. He looks so smart. His hair is beautifully washed. His face is still bruised on one side and his eyes are closed. You touch his hand. He is so cold. Connor holds his mother, and the three of you cry. Your family, but not how it should be.

Sue opens the bag with the gifts you bought for Morgan.
A bottle of beer.
A bottle opener.
A set of Bluetooth speakers.
Some of his sketches.
A can of spray paint.
A family photo of you all on holiday together in Turkey.
Handwritten messages from each of you.
His favourite mug with teabags in it.

You gently place the gifts round him in the coffin where he can reach them. Sue pulls out Morgan's Ray-Bans and

puts them on him. Now he looks just like you always expected him to look whenever he walked through the front door.
The Morgan in your head. Sue remembers how, when he was
little, he always used to say that he felt invisible when he had
sunglasses on. He's not invisible now. For a short while, you
have him back.

There is a knock at the door. It's Daniel. He says the priest
has come to be with you. Father Simon hugs Sue and shakes
Connor's hand. When he gets to you, you feel you have to
warn him.

'Father,' you say, 'I think it's only right I tell you. Morgan
is wearing sunglasses.'

You can hear Morgan laughing and it sounds so good.

Saturday, 5 December 2015

You drop Connor at the railway station. He is playing a gig
tonight in London, and you tell him to give you a text when
he gets there and to have a good time and that he should take
care, and maybe you overdo it, if there is such a thing as that
any more.

Afterwards you go with Sue to the Borough game and
meet Craig and Joe. You fold neatly into the crowd with
Morgan's friends around you, and if anyone is staring
you don't notice. It's a good crowd, plenty of banter, and
occasionally – you're not even sure where from – you hear
someone shout Morgan's name. It streaks into the sky like a
rocket.

At half-time you meet Craig's dad. He's worried about
Craig. He's not been the same since the attack. You see the
way Craig's dad's face folds. Not visible to the eye, but visible
to you, this fold that runs vertically down, through his heart.

His worry about a son. You understand where he's coming from, and later you suggest to Craig and Joe that visiting Morgan might help them. It might replace the last time they saw him in their minds with him at peace. They both say they'd like that, and you say you'll go with them. There is no one else who'll get this privilege – not even your mother, who will ask, and you'll refuse, because you can't be responsible for other people's pain – but they deserve it, these two young men. And Morgan would like it, to look at them through his sunglasses one last time.

In the evening you take Eamon and his friend Zoey to the cinema to see *The Good Dinosaur*. He's fourteen, so you go easy on him. You'll sit on the other side of the cinema if he wants, leave him to it, and his face lights up when you say so. There is no way on earth he won't take you up on that.

So you're there, you and Sue, as the lights dim and the film starts, surrounded by kids, bored, fidgeting, rustling popcorn, needing the toilet every fifteen minutes, and it takes you right back to all the times you did this when your three were young. Bloody hell, you sat through a lot of shit.

It's never easy for the parents of young kids. It's not like herding cats, more like cats and chimps and pigs. There were evenings when you finally got them bathed and into bed, when you slumped down on the sofa barely able to talk and the tiredness felt like radiation in your bones. Days when all you did was field questions you sometimes made up answers to. All those bums you wiped, tears you dried and bruises you kissed, all the while kidding yourself, because that's the only way to survive: if you can just get through the hard bit, then it's plain sailing. Through the tunnel. Out the other side. It'll be so much easier when they start school. When they get older. When they go to work. When they fall in love. All the time unable to admit to yourself it never stops. That worry you feel, it just mutates, but stays tethered to the love that comes with it.

It's a children's film, *The Good Dinosaur*. Just a children's film. But in this film, this silly little film for kids, the mother dinosaur and all her charming young children get into trouble. There is terrible weather, biblical rain, and then a landslide and the smallest one is swept away, and for the rest of the film the mother never stops looking for her son.

You look up in the dark and through your tears see Sue's, trapping tiny balls of light from the screen. No one else can see you, thankfully, but you're both crying and you can't stop. It's comical, really. Bloody stupid. Two grown-ups, surrounded by oblivious children, having a bloody breakdown in a crèche.

You brush yourselves down, so when the lights come up Eamon and Zoey are none the wiser. Whatever level of embarrassment it takes for a teenager to implode is never reached. That's good parenting, what you just did. You've forgotten the billion ways you've made their lives better, but you have.

On the way home you drop off Zoey, then you grab a takeaway and sit down to watch some TV. You're channel-hopping when it comes up on the news that a man has stabbed random people at a Tube station in London. You, Sue and Eamon all look at each other and think the same thing.

'Text Connor,' Eamon says.

It's awful, while you wait for him to answer. Try to stay calm. It's all right. Maybe the show time got pushed back. Maybe the bar is loud so he can't hear his phone. Maybe he's in the toilet. Just think clearly. Think rationally. What would be the chances?

Yeah? Well then why hasn't he—

But then he replies. He's fine. Why are you worrying?

Why? Because that's what you do.

Monday, 7 December 2015

Craig was hesitant to tell you about it, but he thought you should know. He told you about it at the football and you've barely thought of anything else since. Your brain races with it.

Get this.

There's a TV show called *Benefits Britain: Life on the Dole*, on Channel 5. You know the kind of thing. And there is an episode all about Simon Rowbotham, one of the men awaiting trial charged with Morgan's killing. Nobody will believe you when you say this, not now, not in the future, but in all this time that has passed since Morgan died – six weeks now – you've barely thought of these men. There hasn't been room in your head, and they don't deserve a place there. That's for later. For the trial. When Morgan has been laid to rest.

But you think of them now. Despite yourself, you think of them, because Craig says that on the show Simon Rowbotham is giving the camera crew a tour of the area where he lives. And he lives on Meadow Court. In the flats that Morgan and his friends walked past that night. Next to the park where those men who shouted at them ran to attack those boys. Right by the street where Morgan was stabbed.

And you watch it. You don't know why. It will upset Sue if she finds out, you know that.

But you?

You can't turn away.

NARRATOR: *In Benefits Britain, the welfare state is being cut back like never before.*

Simon Rowbotham is wearing a blue-check Lyle & Scott shirt, and a small blue baseball cap, curved to the shape of his head. He's tall, wiry and gaunt, his cheeks sucked tight to his skull. There is no explanation as to why he's carrying a sledgehammer over his shoulder, but in the context of the show it makes a mawkish sense. The producers were looking for people in the process of destruction.

'Reminds me of prison,' he says, standing in the doorway of his bedsit and looking out at the surrounding blocks, pointing at them in turn, 'A wing, B wing, C wing.'

There is a prison-like quality to them, the blocks, the way they impose over Meadow Court, Nuneaton, as though the space between them is an exercise yard. Across from Rowbotham's bedsit is a block with balconies on the other side, and a view over Pool Bank Street Rec.

NARRATOR: *In Benefits Britain, it's reckoned one in five people on out-of-work benefits have done a stretch in prison. And Simon Rowbotham is one of them. At thirty-nine, he's got 113 convictions to his name . . . and counting. But at least he's not done time for a decade or so.*

His bedsit is very small, but he's used to cells so it's no problem. Plug sockets dangle from unplastered walls. His overstuffed rucksack hangs from a nail in the wall next to the fridge, beside the three microwaves stacked one on top of the other that constitute the kitchen. It's cluttered, but Rowbotham has a lot of stuff. A porcelain fairy. A cocktail shaker. A wire-frame candle holder without a candle. Junk, mostly. Things he's found or been given. Not the kind of things he buys. By the time he's paid everything he needs to pay he has around £86 a fortnight to live on. But he takes pride in his clothes. He has over forty designer jackets. A collection of designer baseball caps. A trove of designer jeans, knock-offs probably, but who cares, all out on display for people to see.

NARRATOR: *Si is on probation again, but at least now he's part of a community that isn't behind bars.*
Rowbotham looks out of his doorway, a glint in his eye.

'I run this block,' he says. 'We look after each other round here.'

A MESSAGE FROM THE FUTURE

Maybe you need to hear this now. If you can hear anything, maybe you need to hear this.

In two years' time, in the autumn of 2017 – after the trial of Declan Gray, Karlton Gray and Simon Rowbotham is all finished – you'll do something extraordinary. Something that right now seems unimaginable.

For no reason other than a deep, primal need to understand Morgan's final moments, you'll take a GoPro camera attached to a selfie stick and film yourself walking. You'll walk from the Town Talk pub in Nuneaton, down Bottrill Street, the fastest shortcut into town, and out into Meadow Court, just as Morgan did less than two years before.

On your left you'll see the blocks of flats that comprise Meadow Court.

'I'm not sure whether it's this balcony over here or not,' you'll say, 'but it's one of the balconies in this vicinity, where they were shouted at.'

And then you'll keep walking, retracing Morgan's final steps.

You'll round the corner into Pool Bank Street Rec, slowing slightly.

'They would have walked down here, I believe.'

Someone will shout something indecipherable but vaguely threatening at you, probably for filming yourself, but you won't care. You'll keep going, through the trees that form a patchy tunnel over the leaf-strewn path.

'That's Rowbotham's place,' you'll say, twisting the camera slightly, and thinking perhaps of the documentary that filmed him standing in that very doorway with a sledge-hammer slung over his shoulder. Your brow will wrinkle with the slightest but purest disgust.

You'll keep walking then, through the park out into the car park by the end of the path, not even noticing the man in the ash-coloured tracksuit and white cap who turns to stare at you as you pass, wondering what you're doing no doubt, walking around an area like this with a phone on display for all to see. Maybe he thinks you're mad or foolish or that you don't know what it's like around here, but of course none of those things are true.

At the entrance to the car park, you'll look at the camera and say: 'This is how far away they were attacked,' like a tour guide of your own pain. It'll be two minutes and twenty-six seconds since you passed the balcony, but only if you're walking. Not if you're running. Not if you're chasing somebody. Up over your right shoulder, across the car park, there is a hi-tech CCTV camera overlooking the whole park. In fact, there are cameras everywhere. They weren't there when

Morgan died, but they are now because he did, plasters on deep wounds.

On the corner of Pool Bank Street, by a heavy blue metal gate, you'll stop and look down at the ground like you're caught between now and then.

'This is where Adam was attacked,' you'll say. 'Punched and knocked to the floor by Declan and Karlton, and stabbed, while on the other side of the street behind me, by the white garage, is where Craig was being attacked.'

You'll point down the street a little, to a scene you envisage so vividly it moves across you like a shadow.

'Morgan had walked back to help Craig. He fought Simon off and managed to push Craig forward. Declan and Karlton then ran across to attack Morgan, round about here. This is where the fight ensued . . .'

You'll cross the road to where it happened. A few metres behind you is a big fence behind which the knife used to kill Morgan was found, but, inexplicably, and as you'll learn in court, not until days later. You'll stand there so calmly, in a manner so measured, it'll be beyond the comprehension of those who watch this clip when you upload it to Vimeo that you're standing in the spot where your son was fatally stabbed by men whose steps you've just retraced. And those who do watch will look at your face and see the desire to find out exactly what happened to Morgan that night, burning so fiercely it's hard to look at for long.

Friday, 11 December 2015

Today you bury your child.

Were a parent to name their greatest fear, it would surely be this. But it's bigger than fear. Fear suggests something to be conquered, a mountain in your mind. But there is no terrain to burying a child. Nothing to grip hold of, nothing to find a foothold in. It can't be overcome because it doesn't have a summit. It can't be walked around because it doesn't have edges. It can't be burrowed under because its depth is infinite.

You stand in the kitchen in your new black suit drinking tea and riding waves of dread. Connor comes, then Eamon, both in their new suits, then Sue in a black dress. So smart, the lot of you. You should never have to look as smart as this.

Out of the window you see the car pull up. This is it, then. Instinctively the four of you come together in the lounge, weave your arms round each other's shoulders and waists and huddle like an American football team. You've always hated this kind of thing, but now it hits you what it means. You can do this.

I can't do this.

Daniel knocks on the door, his face etched with sorrow, and you take the slowest drive of your life through the streets of Nuneaton. As you pass, people clasp their hands, close their eyes, dip their heads, as though your pain is being broadcast at a frequency that brings them to a stop.

You know the church is full when you arrive. You can't see the people inside it, can't hear them speak, but there is this overwhelming sensation of a crowd before you join it, of so many anchored hearts. You walk up the aisle through them – 300, maybe 400 people – but you don't see a single one because you're too frightened to lift your head and look at anything other than your reflection in your toecaps, a face so twisted by grief you don't recognise it as your own. The front row is reserved for you, Sue, Connor and Eamon, and as you take your seats Father Simon comes. He greets everybody and then reads the words you wrote for Morgan.

You'd wanted to read them yourself, but Sue convinced you it would be too much. She was right. She is always right.

Funny- Cheeky- Loved to be around friends who made him laugh and giggle. He loved to entertain and never liked hurting anyone. This was Morgan at two years old, the traits that he carried on throughout his life, he never changed did he? He loved his job at the George Eliot Hospital, helping people everyday made him happy.

He loved his weekends out with the boys off to the Boro having a few beers, chanting songs and laughing. There is a theory that Morgan never knew the score at the end of the match! It was all about the fun of it all. Then off down the town more beers and that's how he spent his last day.

On a family holiday to Ireland when Morgan was about nine years old, we were on a beautiful vantage point on the coast which was a religious place dedicated to St Caillin who was a patron saint of fishermen. (pronounced Corleen) There was a religious well which was made out of dry stone walling, Morgan decided to lean on it and he fell through it, the well was semi demolished. Morgan was unharmed but absolutely mortified be the look on his face was priceless. We rebuilt the well and left quickly before anyone noticed. For Morgan's confirmation the following year Morgan chose Caillin as his confirmation name. I'm hoping St Caillin is taking care of him now, maybe taking him fishing. We as a family have been changed forever, we would like to thank Morgan's friends for their care and love they gave him that night he died. We would like to thank the people of Nuneaton for their outpouring of love towards our son and their kindness to us.

It was Dave and Stevie who told you about Morgan's tweet from last September, the month before he died. They hadn't wanted to because it'd upset you – and it did upset you – but really they had no choice:

@morgan_h_one: For my funeral song I want Gypsy by Fleetwood Mac.

Remember when he walked into the lounge and you were playing this record? He was half smirking, half blushing, because you were his dad and no matter what you were doing he could always find a way to be embarrassed by it. Playing air guitar to Fleetwood Mac's 'Gypsy' was guaranteed to do the job. A few weeks later you wanted to listen to it in the truck, but you found the CD was missing. He'd stolen it, the little bugger. And not once did he tell you he loved it just as much as you.

'Gypsy' by Fleetwood Mac, that's the song that's meant to be playing as you lift your son on to your shoulders.

Not like when he was too tired to walk.

Not like when he fell and hurt himself.

The coffin is cool against your neck where his cheek would once have been.

But 'Gypsy' doesn't come on. Instead it's the opening bars of 'Heart of Gold' by Neil Young. It starts, then stops, then starts again, and you look up to see Stevie standing in the pews, mouth wide open in disbelief.

And you? You laugh. You actually laugh. Like it's a trick he played. Like he didn't want it after all. And it helps you. It calms your nerves to know he'd be laughing, so at last you can carry him, out of the church, into the hearse lined with white flowers that spell out MORGAN.

And now you hear it, faint in the distance beneath a duet of crying and birdsong, 'Gypsy', unfurling into the air.

*

81

He did come home. Remember that.

The hearse reverses down the close and stops outside your house. You, Sue, Connor and Eamon stand there for a few minutes in silence, and then you walk behind Morgan back out of the close.

It's important. He did come home.

Everybody is waiting for you at the cemetery, and you all get out of the car the way you said you would, in sunglasses just like Morgan's. The priest says prayers as they lower him into the ground. It's such a long way down. There is a thread between you and the coffin, and the further it goes the more you unravel. You throw in four white roses and then you are undone.

When you arrive at the wake, everyone is waiting. What do you say to a room full of tear-streaked faces? Expectation moves through it like weather.

'It's OK to laugh,' you say. 'And it's OK to cry.'

Everybody watches the film Joe has made, with all the footage you gave him of Morgan and Connor as children doing magic shows, and him painting, and their band playing, and him smiling as he put the finishing touches to another GRUT. Everyone is sobbing. It's a beautiful video, but it's all too much.

Afterwards you sit with family and you talk, and the video plays on a loop, Morgan's life repeating, over and over, until 5 p.m. comes and goes and it's just a few of you left in the bar, the staff included, all crying, watching it a final time.

What a boy. A credit to you. What a good young man.

You leave before they switch it off. In your head it plays forever.

AN INCOMPLETE LIST OF THINGS YOU NO LONGER KNOW HOW TO DO

How to book a family holiday.
How to take a family photo.
How to set the table for a family dinner.
How to have a family Christmas.
How to stop.

Justice

Monday, 14 December 2015

Since the funeral you've felt nothing but thick, black sadness. Today, though, you feel something new. You make tea, sit down, open up the paper that's been lying around the place since last week, and you are overcome with an intense and fiery rage:

> A crime crackdown in Nuneaton has seen police arrest 13 people for a variety of offences linked to burglaries, drug-dealing and theft. Operation Offa was launched by police in response to residents' concerns in the Manor and Abbey Green areas of the town.
>
> It comes just a few weeks after George Eliot Hospital worker Morgan Hehir, aged 20, suffered fatal injuries in Pool Bank Recreational Park, in Nuneaton, on Halloween.
>
> Declan Jay Gray, 20, and Karlton Mark Gray, 18, both of Waverley Square, Nuneaton, and Simon Valentine Rowbotham, 39, of Meadow Street, Nuneaton, have all been charged with murder and are currently on remand in prison.

At the start of December, almost exactly a month after Morgan's death, a group of officers were brought together to target offenders highlighted by the community.

They are working with other organisations, including Nuneaton and Bedworth Borough Council, to tackle anti-social behaviour, drug use or supply, handling stolen goods, theft, vehicle crime and burglary.

SAM DIMMER, *Coventry Evening Telegraph*,
6 December 2015

You're angry. Of course you're angry. The police are trying to reassure the public that the area is safe weeks after Morgan was stabbed to death, that they're suppressing the criminal network plaguing those streets, and it feels like an insult, like a single stitch on an axe wound, all too fucking late. You grab a pen from the kitchen junk drawer and write down all the times Morgan was a victim of crime in the last two years, in the order the crimes occurred.

Two bikes stolen.
Front wheel of bike stolen.
Beaten.
Stabbed to death.
Phone and wallet stolen.

And you wonder. Are we as safe as we think we are, here in Treacle Town?

A TRAGEDY IN NUNEATON: PART TWO
THE DEATH OF ADRIAN HOWARD

Adrian Howard was simply doing what he always seemed to be doing, walking through Nuneaton, minding his own business. This was his home town. He'd lived his life here.

Now thirty-eight, he had two sons, and owned a mobile fast-food business selling sandwiches and snacks to a faithful clientele he often got to know by name. But that was across the other side of town from where he found himself on the chilly evening of 14 October 2010, with everything about to change.

Adrian had been visiting friends and having a few drinks before heading home along Black-A-Tree Road, which is shaped like a horseshoe nailed to the town's hoof. He was almost there when he came across a fifteen-year-old boy, who'd also spent the afternoon drinking. The boy, who with hair cropped close to his scalp and an urgent gait looked like most boys around these parts, approached Adrian and asked for a cigarette. Adrian, because he had none or didn't want to share them with a child, felt that he had to refuse, and did. Then he tried to make his way home.

But the boy still wanted one of Adrian's cigarettes. When Adrian denied him again, the boy punched him twice in the face, so hard that it knocked him to the ground. Then the boy kicked Adrian. Then the boy stamped on Adrian, who was lying on the pavement, now unconscious and unable to stop the furious assault that showed no sign of abating.

Across the road, a pensioner heard the commotion. She rose from her chair as fast as she could and went to the window. It wasn't altogether unusual to see trouble round here. This was just one of those areas, and Nuneaton had a few. Most people were broke, there were high levels of unemployment, and these streets were no stranger to police intervention. Hardness, or rather the willingness to fight, had given some of her neighbours an ominous local celebrity status that had once so scared the local paperboy he'd purposely skipped their houses. But though the pensioner had seen many things while peeking from behind the curtain, she'd seen nothing of this ferocity before. It was the pensioner's husband who, after joining her at the window, raised the alarm. But by the time the police and an ambulance arrived the boy was long gone, and no one could say where to.

If the boy's mother saw him return home after the attack took place, that's not what she told police. In fact, she corroborated the alibi he gave them when he was arrested a couple of days later. That he couldn't have attacked Adrian Howard on Black-A-Tree Road on the evening in question because he'd been home with his mother since 6.30 p.m.

Adrian had already spent a few nights in hospital by the time the boy's mother was making her statement. The attack was so brutal it had left him with multiple injuries, including bleeding around the brain. He would be in hospital for a few weeks more, before eventually being discharged. But he wasn't home for long. On 4 December, a blood clot in his leg became detached and travelled to his heart. Adrian went into cardiac arrest in the town centre and died. The post-mortem showed that the injuries he sustained in the attack made a significant contribution to his death.

Though the boy was charged with murder and was due to stand trial, his plea of guilty to a lesser charge of manslaughter was accepted because the judge said he had a 'lack of intent' to cause serious harm. Defending QC Michael Burrows said: 'He was fifteen and a half at the time, with a borderline level of intellectual function and a childhood deprived of good parenting and role models.' The judge added: 'On this fateful night you were in a bad temper and drunk, so angry that you were an emotional time-bomb.'

Appearing at the Crown Court in Leamington, the boy was sentenced to four and a half years for Adrian's manslaughter. A jury also found his thirty-five-year-old mother guilty of perverting the course of justice by providing police with a false statement to support her son's false alibi. She was sentenced to two years in prison.

The explosive and vicious attack that killed Adrian Howard was chalked up to a behavioural blip, something the boy should be rehabilitated from in under five years. As such, Adrian had merely been in the wrong place at the wrong time. He had turned a corner in the town where he'd worked, where he'd raised children, where he'd lived his life, only to have it ended by something resembling bad luck. But the boy's behaviour was not an anomaly. As Adrian must have known when he looked into the boy's eyes before he slipped into unconsciousness, violence was a part of him. This wouldn't be the last time the boy let it show.

Monday, 4 January 2016

Only now can you bring yourself to read all the text messages you received at midnight on New Year's Eve.

Hope you have the best new year ever!
Wishing you a very happy new year!
2016 is your year, I can feel it!

You feel like replying, out of pettiness, out of spite. You even run your fingers across the letters on the screen and imagine yourself responding:

Of course we will!
Thanks for your kind thoughts!
Roll on 2016! It's going to be amazing!

But no one understands your situation, and no one can be expected to. No one except Sue, who looks at you like you're an Olympic gold-medal-winning miserable bugger, because you're seriously irritating her and have been for a while. The hangover isn't helping. You can still feel it lingering, even after the weekend is over. They're not easy to shift at your age, and staying up until 5 a.m. on New Year's Eve demolishing a bottle of sambuca (horrendous, yes, but perfect – this was always Morgan's favourite poison, so much so that his favourite pub banned him from drinking it) while you sat around listening to records and telling stories about him probably wasn't the best idea you've ever had.

You've been under Sue's feet for two months now. It's time to get back to work. To be whatever version of Colin Hehir exists between now and the trial. Though the mere thought of returning becomes fear as it moves through your mind.

You meet your boss, Katie, in the main part of the building to hand over your sick note from the doctor. This little bit of paper, a receipt for your pain. Everyone here knows what happened, just like everyone in the town knows what happened. It's left a mark on you. She's good though, Katie. She asks if you want to go down to the transport office, maybe stay a while, have a chat with a few of the blokes, put the kettle on. That kind of thing. The stuff you used to do.

You've never really felt panic before. Not like this. Not a panic that picks you up and wrings you out. But it comes now, as you open the door of the transport office and step inside. It grips and twists and tries to tear you in two. You wonder if anyone else can see its tight hands round your middle. If the couple of drivers in there who are starting their shift do, they don't show it. They see you and smile and they pour you a coffee and for a while you just sit and talk shit. You discuss nothing of what has happened, but you don't need to talk about Morgan for them to feel the agony you're in. You can see it on their faces. They've got children too.

The occupational-health team member looks like a doctor in his shirt and tie. You don't see many of them around here. He's upright and expectant, with a firm, officious handshake that in any other context might feel reassuring, but instead just reminds you why you're here.

'Take a seat,' he says. 'It's important you know I haven't been given any detail . . . but you have been off work since 2 November. This is confidential, though you don't have to give me any details if you don't want to.'

But you do. You do want to. So you tell him everything. About Morgan. His murder. The sorrow that has swallowed your household. How you can't even do Christmas any more. How it used to be a turkey dinner with all the trimmings and everybody there: crackers, hats, jokes worse than yours, so much food you all collapsed on the sofa together afterwards and moaned about who took up most space. How this year you had a sad-looking Christmas ready meal, a turkey in a tray with all the vegetables on the side from the supermarket that you could just bung in the oven without thinking, and Sue only got out of bed to eat it, and she did that while crying and the kids sat in silence to let her. Next Christmas you'll have curry in an Indian restaurant. Sprout bhaji with turkey tikka.

Because that's your 'new normal'. That's what *they* call it, not what you call it. Your new normal. Like it's a positive, like it's a choice, a hobby you've taken up or a new coat you wear, instead of you no longer being able to do the things you cherished most about your life. Like Christmas. You always loved Christmas. But everything you love is now in the past tense.

The man looks back at you, his demeanour suddenly different, as though you've warped him, like wood under water, his head dipping lower the more you speak. And you're sorry, of course you are. You didn't mean to upset him. You didn't want to give him a horrible half-hour he'll go home and tell his wife about when she asks why his face is ashen, the answers he gives short and quiet. But you want everyone to know what you've been through. What Christmas means to you from now on.

'OK,' he says after a silence that stretches for miles. 'How about you come back and sweep up in the yard to start with? To phase you back into work.'

'I can't do that,' you say. 'It would give me too much time to think.'

'OK,' he says, 'OK.'

Katie helps you arrange to start slowly, in a week's time, but still by doing your job, delivering stock to supermarkets. Just a few local ones at first, until you find your feet. Maybe begin by going with your friend John.

The new normal.

Tuesday, 12 January 2016

He's not what people think lorry drivers are like, is John. He's very intelligent. He reads books (not at the wheel, mind). He doesn't watch *Top Gear*. There are no scars on his hands from the dragging of his knuckles. He's got half a brain all right. You liked him from the moment you met him.

He's there to make sure you're coping, and it's reassuring to have him with you. As the day goes on you confide in him about what has happened, and he listens more than he talks, which is exactly what you need, because it keeps coming out of you and it wants soaking up.

'It would have been sad,' he says.

'What would?' you say.

'Seeing you walking round the yard, sweeping up with a broom. It would have been heartbreaking.'

You nod.

'So how did I do?' you say.

He looks confused.

'What?'

'How did I do on my first day back at work?'

He laughs for a good long while, and the sound of it is warm and full, like the bong of a well-struck bell.

'I didn't notice any problems,' he says. 'You'll be fucking fine.'

Thursday, 28 January 2016

Waiting for the trial of your son's killers is like looking up the mountain at the boulder you know must fall. Right now it is teetering, but soon it will topple, and it will hurtle unstoppably towards you. And a part of you wants it to. You want this to end, so much, and it can't begin to end until you get justice. There can be no relief. But you can't make it come. And so you must find a way to live until it does. You must work.

It's like therapy, work. If you believed in mantras – you never used to, but maybe now you do – this would be the one that gets you up every morning.

It's like therapy, work.

The more you do it – climbing in the cab, eating up the miles – the less you have to deal with the stuff you have to deal with. You are the truck and your grief is the road. Keep moving. Just keep moving.

Olivia warned you work would be tiring when you went back. And she was right, it is. Extraordinarily so. In a way it's never been before. Sometimes you're halfway back from Peterborough with your head nodding like a busted mario-nette, and the pull of the bed in the back of the cab is almost too much to resist. But there is beauty in keeping busy. Paying the bills. Keeping a roof over your family's heads. You're traditional like that. It's what you're meant to do.

It catches you out though, sometimes. Like when you're in the cab on your break, playing that silly little golf game on your phone, and the computer-generated golfer, coinci-dentally named Morgan, pops up to show you his swing. Or right now, when you're driving along, somewhere between home and Birmingham as it seems you always are, becalmed by the mesmeric trundle of the tyres, and a familiar song comes on the radio.

Do you hear it? That picky guitar. The lush harmony swelling beneath it. Her voice, its vulnerability and strength.

'That was "Gypsy", by Fleetwood Mac, of course, written by Stevie Nicks and released in 1982, from the number-one album *Mirage* . . .'

And you, a big, butch lorry driver, suddenly with so many tears in your eyes you can barely see the road ahead.

But you like crying. Every time it happens you let it out, and it feels good. You try to imagine Morgan in the passen-ger seat, watching over you. You hope to catch him there, through the prism of a tear in the corner of your eye.

A couple of weeks back you read something in the paper about another bereaved father feeling his dead son by his side. Remembering this now, high up in the cab, you bristle with jealousy. You want this too. You want Morgan, beside you. But you're struggling to feel his presence, and you're scared it is gone. What if to lose that is to lose him again?

Saturday, 6 February 2016

Craig comes round. He wants to show you something. You get in the car, and it moves through Nuneaton like a tin opener, peels back its sharp and rusty lid, shows you something inside you didn't know was there.

Turns out Morgan's art is all around you. GRUT beneath the tree on the wall behind the supermarket. GRUT under the bridge in the park. GRUT on the sides of decrepit warehouses. GRUT writ large beside the railway tracks. The town where he lived had been his gallery, and you'd never really known.

You have your camera, and as Craig tells you the story behind every piece, about all the fun stuff they did together, the good times they had making art, you take photographs. It's all temporary, this. These walls could be painted over or cleaned up or knocked down any minute. Be baked by sun and beat by wind until they simply crumble into dust. But you'll always have these pictures of the art Morgan made, and though you can't know it yet, they will bring you tremendous comfort for the rest of your life. GRUT FOREVER.

Friday, 12 February 2016

Oh Colin. Look at you. Waking up suddenly in a you-shaped puddle of sweat. You can tell the trial date is nearing because this happens more and more, like when you receive a little update from Alan. Or like today, when you need to be somewhere, smartly dressed in a shirt and tie you knot while you wonder exactly what you'll feel – rage? emptiness? an impossible sadness? – when Declan Gray, Karlton Gray and Simon Rowbotham finally open their mouths to speak. Today is the day you'll hear their pleas.

Get used to waiting. There will be a load of this when the trial starts. Countless hours of sitting in the comfortable blue chairs behind the witness-protection doors, through which arrive an apparently endless train of biscuits.

Sue hasn't been before, so one of the volunteers takes you round the court for a tour and you go with her to hold her hand, even though it's your second time. He must be in his seventies, the guide, but he's as enthusiastic as a Labrador puppy.

'This is where the judge sits, this is where the jury sits, and in the bullet-proof room over here is where the defendants will be seated.' He's smiling. The man loves his job. In fact, he barely stops talking. There's a distinct possibility he speaks more in ten minutes than you and Sue have since you met.

'You can be sworn in with the Koran if Christianity's not your thing, or if you're an atheist there are words for you too.'

Hang on a minute. Is he ever going to shut up? It's not a guided tour of the Natural History Museum. You're not paying bloody customers. You want to grab him and scream: *Do you have any idea why we're here?!*

But you don't do that. Of course you don't. Instead you suffer in silence, eat two more biscuits than you really ought to, and you wait some more.

When it finally happens, you're up in the bird's nest above it all again, out of view. They still haven't fixed the dodgy

TV. But it's through that grainy, flickering twelve inches of screen you watch the three men shuffle into court. The judge asks them how they plead to the murder of your son.

And it's just words, isn't it? Just words in the mouths of men.

Simon Valentine Rowbotham, you have been charged with the murder of Morgan James Francis Hehir. How do you plead?

Not guilty.

Karlton Mark Gray, you have been charged with the murder of Morgan James Francis Hehir. How do you plead?

Not guilty.

That's what you thought they'd say, because they're trying to distance themselves from their parts in the attack that killed Morgan. It's self-preservation. After all, they weren't the ones with the knife. Declan Gray had the knife.

Declan Jay Gray, you have been charged with the murder of Morgan James Francis Hehir. How do you plead?

Guilty, to manslaughter.

Right now you feel nothing, and maybe you won't until the trial, which is more than three months away. Maybe you won't feel anything until you get what you need. You need justice the way you need air.

A NICE DREAM

A room. The wallpaper is patterned, brown and beige with hints of orange. A cloud of cigarette smoke moves like a flock of starlings. In the centre is a teak coffee table. Standing around the table are six or seven old people, talking. Their conversations lapse and fudge until one is indistinguishable from the next. They are mostly drinking beer, all from glass tankards, smiling as they bring them together with a satisfying clink.

Suddenly, a young man charges into the room through a door that didn't exist before but appeared just for him. He is kicking a small yellow football, moving quickly as he dribbles it through the legs of the people in the room. He dips left, fades right, and with a surge of pace crashes into the legs of a man whose face turns immediately red.

'You stupid little idiot,' he says to the back of the boy's head as the boy disappears, laughing, through the door by which he came in.

Thursday, 3 March 2016

'It was Morgan,' you say, 'in the dream.' Olivia sits in the corner chair of the conservatory, nodding and listening. She deals with people like you for a living, and it's just as well because you're lost. 'And the people he was annoying, the ones who were complaining about him, they were from my dad's family, but they've all passed away from old age.'

She doesn't need to ask you how it made you feel. She knows you'll tell her anyway.

'That was him all over. He had that effect on most of us while he was alive, with his sense of humour, and wanting to be at the heart of everything going on. And the funny thing is, to see him in my dream was . . . nice.'

She smiles. Must be the first time she's heard that word come out of your mouth. But then your eyes dim because you're not in that room any more, with the wallpaper and the smoke and him.

What could you have done differently? You shouldn't ask yourself that question, but you do, though the answer is nothing and always will be. There is nothing you could have done differently that means Morgan would be alive now. He was a young man for God's sake. He'd a mind of his own, a life of his own. What were you meant to do? Stop him going out to see his friends? Chain him to a radiator? What life would that have been?

But the question goes round and round in your head regardless. And it always brings you to the same place. What if there was something you could have done after all?

In the summer before he died, Morgan and Craig went on holiday to Newquay to stay with Joe. The beach was long and golden. They sat on sand that glowed pink in the dusk, drinking beers, laughing, taking photographs. He was the happiest he'd ever been.

When he came home afterwards he sat down beside you on the sofa, and with his eyes wide open he told you he had a plan, a brilliant plan, a plan for how his life would play out. He was going to move to the sea, to Newquay. Answer a calling. Stay at Joe's place and get a job.

And you shook your head. Not angry. Fatherly. Your instinct was to put him off. How could he just up sticks and move to Newquay? He didn't have any money. And anyway, was it fair to impose on Joe like that? Having a mate to stay and gaining a lodger are hardly the same thing. Maybe he should do it next year. Get a job in Nuneaton first. Save up a bit. Give it some thought.

What could you have done differently? You could never have given him that advice. That way he'd still be alive.

'I think you have post-traumatic stress disorder,' Olivia says.

Me?

You thought PTSD was for people in war zones. Soldiers who'd been shot at. Men who pulled their brothers out of fires. But that's the thing about trauma. It won't reveal itself to you. It's not in your mind, it's hiding behind it.

Thursday, 31 March 2016

Alan is driving you to the Magistrates' Court in Leamington for the trial of Miroslav Holan, the man accused of stealing Morgan's iPhone and wallet as he lay dying in the street, when he ends a lull in normal everyday conversation about nothing much in particular to tell you that Holan has pleaded guilty to disposing of the stolen items, but not to stealing them.

You've been told so little about this by the police, and it's all been so dwarfed by the murder investigation and the trial of Morgan's killers, that for a second you struggle to understand what it is Alan's telling you. He explains it again, but it still won't go in. Understandable, really. Hard to make sense of anything in a world where Morgan's iPhone and wallet could be taken but not stolen and then dumped while he lay dying.

'What do you mean, he's pleaded guilty to disposing of the items?'

'Holan says he picked up Morgan's iPhone and wallet and tried to give them to a police officer when they arrived. But he claims the policeman told him to go away, so he disposed of them.'

'Where?'

'I don't know.'

The car turns off the motorway and slows, but your mind still races. All you can think about is the police you saw lifting the drain cover outside Lidl. If they were acting on information from Holan, did it mean he'd told them that's where he'd disposed of the wallet and phone? And as they weren't found, are you supposed to believe they'd just been washed away?

'But Joe . . . Joe said when he went to help Morgan there was a man going through Morgan's pockets, and he offered him Morgan's driving licence and the next thing he was gone.' You can hear the anger rising in your voice, which means Alan can hear it too, and Sue in the back, who hasn't said anything but is still somehow quieter than before. 'That's stealing. And it took the police weeks to find him. How come this has been accepted?'

Alan shakes his head.

'I don't know why the CPS have accepted it,' he says, 'but it's what he has admitted to.'

You'd leap up if you could. Leap up and smash your head through the roof of the car.

'This is a load of shit! He stole them! He stole them and panicked after Morgan died!'

'I don't know,' Alan says, 'but you might be right,' and you can tell he agrees with you even though he's not allowed to say as much.

You head into the court and there's a two-hour wait before the two detectives in charge of the theft case flop into the seats opposite you in the way so many men with bad news have these past few months. You've developed quite a nose for bad news, can spot on sight the sorry mouths it's about to escape. There is a part of you becoming immune.

This, though, this shocks you. Miroslav Holan has not turned up for court.

What?

They're going to put out a warrant to have him arrested.

How fearlessly some people must live. You lose sleep if you get a reminder for the gas bill. You get tension headaches if you forget to call someone back. But some people exist outside the constraints of decency, duty and promises. They float above what's right and wrong. If they're not scared of letting someone down, not scared of causing someone pain, not scorn, not shame, not even prison, what is it they are scared of?

It's another long wait before Alan returns, sheepishly this time, which isn't his usual style.

'So . . . they can't arrest him.'

'What?' you say.

'He was given the wrong date by his solicitor,' Alan says. 'He turned up yesterday instead.'

It's true. They checked the court's CCTV. There he is, clear as day, Miroslav Holan arriving for his trial a whole day early. Coming in and then going home again, probably unable to believe his bloody luck.

'He can't afford to come back today,' Alan says. He's apologetic, upset even, same as you.

'So what will happen now?'

'Well, it looks like they'll have to reschedule.'

You watch Miroslav Holan's interpreter put their book into their bag, slide their jacket on and walk out into a crisp spring afternoon.

You always took comfort in the systems and institutions that exist to help and protect you. Otherwise, how would you ever have dared send your sons out into the world? Without the belief these institutions will fold around you when you come to harm, or mete out justice when it needs meting out in your name, both sanity and society would collapse. But it requires more than belief – it requires blind and foolish faith – to remove oneself from the fact that the moving parts of the machines we put in place are human, and that humans are fallible. And that just one mistake, on top of another, on top of another, might one day destroy the lives they were designed to hold sacrosanct. The lives of good people. Lives like yours.

Tuesday, 5 April 2016

Maybe it's because you've been in enough courts now, but you can tell people's roles by the clothes they wear. Grieving parents, that's an easy one. Sue's in a simple black trouser suit. Black suits and plain ties are detectives. Flamboyant stripes or check suits with pinks or pastel shades are barristers, perhaps because they have to put on a show. The tracksuit? That's him. That's Miroslav Holan.

The room is small, oppressively so, like the little American courts you sometimes see on TV. Low, swinging gates divide it in two so you can sit at the back, while on the other side are the solicitors, subdivided left and right into prosecution and defence. The magistrates' section is raised up and speaks of power. Not as high as in Crown Court, where they're up on a plinth, but high enough for you to know who is in charge, whose decision on Holan's sentence you're waiting so desperately to hear you barely notice how your fingers leave milky-white pressure prints in the flesh of Sue's hand.

All rise.

The three magistrates come and take their places, and Alan leans closer, whispering a live commentary of events into your ear as they unfold.

'The magistrates are all volunteers,' he says, 'it's the one sitting beneath the magistrates who has all the knowledge. He's the legal beagle.'

'Hang on a minute,' you say, 'which one's our solicitor?' You haven't met him. How can you not have met him?

Alan points across the court to a small, older man with a gentle face and soft edges. Next to the solicitor on the other side – a strong-looking woman who reminds you of a headmistress who used to terrify you when she was pissed off with you, which she kind of always was – he looks more like Alan Bennett than the harbinger of justice you were hoping for.

Miroslav Holan stands on the left of the magistrates with a listening device and the interpreter, who comes to life as Holan's solicitor starts to make his case.

He's admitted to disposing of Morgan's phone and wallet. And his guilty plea has been accepted. So you won't hear what he says happened with Morgan today. This is just about sentencing. But out of nowhere, and despite his client not having to speak and give you the answers you crave, Holan's solicitor says it's worth pointing out his client remembers the day well, because on Saturday, 31 October 2015 Miroslav Holan was having the best day of his life. The same day that would become the worst of yours.

It was a brilliant and memorable day for Holan because just that morning he had become a father. Later, while his girlfriend stayed with the baby, he'd gone out with a friend in their car to get some drinks to celebrate. And that's when it happened. The event he so deeply regrets. Not stealing Morgan's stuff, because he didn't do that, Holan's solicitor says. He found it and tried to give it to a policeman but was turned away. No, the event he so deeply regrets is disposing of it later.

Not that Holan came forward to tell police he'd disposed of it after seeing the press attention regarding Morgan's murder. On the contrary. The only reason Holan was caught at all is because the car he was travelling in that night was picked up by vehicle-registration cameras in Nuneaton town centre a few weeks later. And when the police knocked on his friend's door to make inquiries about what he'd been doing driving by a murder scene, the man gave them Holan's name and address straight away.

You stare at Holan for five minutes, maybe ten. But he won't make eye contact. You're not looking for vengeance. You're looking for remorse. You want it to tumble out of him. For him to feel your hurt, and to show you that he's sorry. You can't move past the thought that this man saw Morgan as he lay dying. He was there with him when you were not. And for a second you wonder if you'd swap places with him right now, and stare down the barrel of a prison sentence, if it meant you could have rested a hand on Morgan's head in those final moments and told him it was going to be OK.

Your solicitor, who you were automatically assigned and who you've never bloody met, rises from his seat to read your Victim Personal Statement. It's only short, but you spent ages writing it, melted yourself down and poured yourself into it. You squeeze Sue's hand hard before he begins, and you mouth the words as he says them, this man you've never met, speaking for you.

'I feel so sickened by the vulture who stole from my son Morgan . . .' he begins. Except – wait a minute – these aren't your words, are they? He's skipping bits. Missing lines. There's a nonchalance to his delivery, as though he's been asked to repeat the punchline to a joke nobody got, and it makes you so angry you turn puce, like you're ripening.

You can barely take in the conversation in the courtroom afterwards. But you can see it's bad. Alan is shaking his head.

'What's going on, Alan?' you say. And he tells you. There are reports that need to be done before sentencing that should have been done already, about Holan and his girlfriend and their baby and their needs and their well-being. That's when the penny drops. That's why Holan's solicitor said all that shit earlier about it being the best day of Holan's life. That's why you all had to sit in court this morning to find out he'd become a father on the day your son was murdered. Because Holan's team know it will be considered when it comes to his sentencing. It was a bid for sympathy. A call for clemency. Do they think you're stupid? Some little man who will come in and listen and won't ask questions? That you'll just roll over and take it?

'What the hell?' you say, too loud for a courtroom probably. 'What about Morgan's wallet and phone?'

Court is adjourned and you're taken back to the waiting room, where you want to dash the biscuits across the fucking floor. Sue's got calm-down eyes, but she's angry too, you can see it and feel it. It burns.

'I'm not happy with the solicitor either,' you say to Alan. 'He hasn't even talked to us and he skipped through my VPS like it didn't matter, like it was a bloody shopping list he couldn't be arsed with. He is paid to care, but what was that back there? It looked like he couldn't give a toss!'

Alan nods, looks down at the ground around his feet.

'OK,' he says. 'I'll report back for you.'

Good. You want to be heard.

Friday, 8 April 2016

It takes them three days to complete Holan's pre-sentencing reports that should already have been done, and when you arrive back at court to hear his fate you find a whole new prosecution solicitor, magicked out of thin air, walking towards you with his hand outstretched. He apologises for your VPS not being read properly last time.

'Would you like to read it yourself today?'

You're not a public speaker. You never have been, other than your wedding speech and that lasted, what, two minutes? Then it was all to the bar. It's not that you're nervous. Well, you are a bit. You used to run a chip shop and now you drive trucks for a living. You're not Laurence Olivier.

It's more the words. They're not always there. Not all of them, not in the right order. But then you think of what you used to say to Morgan when he asked you to fix his bike and you couldn't be bothered. *If a job's worth doing, it's worth doing yourself.*

You're attuned to it now, that wisp of sadness you put in people's eyes. He's read your VPS, the new prosecution solicitor says, and it made him cry. If one of your family had said that to you, you'd have thought they were taking the piss or something. But this guy? OK. Maybe you do have something to say after all.

So you do. You go in there and you stand up and you get ready to speak when instructed. You tell the court about the impact the theft of Morgan's iPhone and wallet in his dying moments has had on you and your family.

He'd be so proud of you, you know.

'I feel so sickened by the vulture who stole from my son Morgan. You saw an opportunity to strike for your own gain . . .'

Miroslav Holan raises his hand, and through his translator says he's having problems with his hearing device.

So you shuffle your weight from foot to foot, take a deep breath and start again.

'I feel so sickened by the vulture who stole from my son Morgan. You saw an opportunity to strike for your own gain . . .'

His hand goes up again. Not yet.

Stay calm.

Wait.

He'd be so proud of you.

Go on.

'I feel so sickened by the vulture who stole from my son Morgan. You saw an opportunity to strike for your own gain and had no problem in this terrible act of inhumanity. The taking of his phone and the photographs contained have been denied to us, stealing part of his legacy to us. It comes as a final blow to us as a family that in our loved son's life that he should have a violent death, but that was not enough, he was robbed, when he was so very vulnerable and wounded, it was the final insult to our son Morgan. He didn't deserve this. Morgan was a caring person, he worked at the NHS to help others and he was worthy of being cared for in return.'

You leave a silence afterwards. Let them all exist in it, as you must.

The magistrate looks around the room to check that everyone's ready. You fill your lungs with air that feels like dust.

Eighteen weeks in prison, she says. Eighteen weeks, reduced to twelve weeks, suspended for twelve months. It would not be appropriate to pay compensation, except for £135 in costs, and an £80 court surcharge.

Another magistrate looks at you and shakes his head in disgust.

'Mr Holan,' she says, 'you are free to leave the court.' And almost immediately, that is what he does.

'What the fuck was that, Alan?' you say. 'The fucking justice system? He's just going to walk away, same as he did when he came on the wrong fucking day? Where is the phone? Where is the wallet? Where's all the stuff that got stolen off a dying man? Why would it not be appropriate to pay compensation?'

Alan doesn't look up.

'Morgan is dead,' he says. 'How can he pay him?'

'Well that stinks,' you say. 'It fucking stinks.'

'I know,' says Alan. 'I know.'

The new prosecution solicitor walks in pulling a large leather bag on wheels behind him. He just wants to say goodbye, and good luck going forward. He's got a big smile on his face.

'Are you happy with how that all went?' you say.

'Yes,' he says, 'very.'

And then he leaves to catch his train.

Later you prop your bike against a wall, take off your helmet, unzip your fluorescent yellow jacket and you search. You walk up and down Pool Bank Street, checking every hedge, every scrub, every manhole cover you can find for Morgan's iPhone and wallet. You get down on your knees and you search until the road leaves prints on your hands and your joints swell and you ache with it twofold, you ache from the searching and you ache with the loss.

But you find nothing.

AN INCOMPLETE LIST OF THINGS PEOPLE SAY THAT CAN'T BE ANSWERED

He would be looking down on you now, smiling.

Time is a healer.

Can you feel his presence?

I can't imagine what it's like.

Tiny steps.

Baby steps.

You're doing so well.

You've been in our prayers.

This kind of thing shouldn't happen to families like yours.

One day at a time.

How's Sue?

Saturday, 9 April 2016

Oh, there you are. On the bed, sallow-skinned, fingers screwed into the mattress, Tommy-gun heartbeat and sweat speckling the sheets. Sue walks in, looks you up and down.

'You coming?'

You can't imagine standing up. Pulling on your trousers. Putting one foot in front of the other to even get as far as the door. You're riddled with fear. Rigid with it.

'I don't know,' you say.

Right now, she's the strong one. You alternate, like your pain is a see-saw with one of you on each end, taking turns to be up and down. The thing you want most is to be in the middle, with her, at the same time. But it never really happens.

Kirsty is Sue's friend. Her husband Frankie signed up for a fourteen-mile charity run. It was only when he got accepted that he found out it was actually forty miles. As bad news goes it doesn't compare to yours, but that doesn't mean it's not bad news. Frankie has never run anything like that far in his life. Once he stopped laughing, and quite possibly crying, he came through with a fierce determination to turn his accidentally lengthy ordeal into something good – to raise money for George Eliot Hospital in Morgan's name. It was a beautiful gesture, and they decided, with your and Sue's blessing, to hold a race night. But now it's here and you're welded to the bed.

'You'd better make your bloody mind up,' Sue says. 'We've got to go.'

You reluctantly fold your body into a suit, already formulating a plan. If you take a GoPro camera with you and hide behind that, it might look like you're doing something useful, rather than hoping nobody will chat to you more than you've ever hoped for anything. It's just a shame cameras got so small.

There's a large screen at the front of the hall with horse races projected on to it. Beneath that a team of volunteers sit taking cash bets from the people at the tables, which are all themed with things Morgan liked to drink. Stella Stallions, Peroni Ponies, that kind of thing. There are loads of people here to support and you recognise most of them. Morgan's friends, colleagues, family acquaintances. You enter and they turn towards you, as though you are framed and hung.

They mean well. They come and talk to you. They're trying to help you, and you appreciate that, of course. But they want you to be *you* again. Happy, smiling Colin Hehir. Would do anything for anyone, Colin Hehir. Always up for a laugh, Colin Hehir. But the truth is, that's what's been taken from you, not just a son. You no longer exist.

'How's Sue?' That's the worst question. Do they want you to tell them how she really is? Could they handle it? Should they know?

Once, before all this, you were driving your truck late one evening and listening to a radio phone-in about meeting your heroes. Something about the voices of strangers carried you through the night, a reminder that somewhere out there in the darkness others were also awake. A man called in to say he'd been in a club in Manchester in the early 1980s when he saw Morrissey and Johnny Marr of The Smiths at the bar, perhaps toasting the beginning of their meteoric rise to stardom. The man loved The Smiths. Johnny Marr's guitar gave him immense joy, but Morrissey's lyrics spoke to him in a way no other music did. He was on the verge of an all-consuming idolatry that, on facing Morrissey alone as Marr went to the toilet, robbed him of all he had to say. But still he opened his mouth, and Morrissey waited gamely to hear what would emerge.

'Was that Johnny Marr?' the man said to his god.

'Yeah,' Morrissey said to his wounded disciple. And that was that, a brief conversation that haunted the man enough to call a radio phone-in decades later, hoping for an exorcism.

What is it about human nature that makes it easier to ask how the other, absent half is, rather than confront what's in front of them? Why don't they ask how you're doing? Sometimes you look into their eyes and you can tell that's what they really want to know. And then what? You do your usual schtick. You tell them how you really feel and what actually happened and their face melts into horror, and you realise too late you've given them a fraction of your pain to hold. Not much, but enough. And it is heavy, so heavy it's difficult to carry. You're hurting them now and you feel shit for doing it, but unless you keep your mouth shut, what else is there to do? That's all that comes out of it these days. Not words. Just pain.

'How's Sue?' they ask.

'Oh, you know,' you say, turning a little, holding up your camera as though across the room there is something you urgently need to record. There's such relief on their faces when you say it, though.

'Oh, you know.' Yeah, that works. That works for now.

They raise £4,000 for the hospital, and you're honoured and humbled, but the biggest smile, the real one, won't come for a few years yet. One day in the future, Frankie will send you a photograph of himself in one of two huge reclining chairs in the Day Procedures Unit at George Eliot Hospital, chairs that this money bought, with little brass plaques that say 'In Memory Of Morgan' on them. In the photograph he's relaxing in the chair his surprise forty-mile run paid for, having just had a vasectomy. If anyone deserves to lower their aching testicles into a comfy seat, it's him.

Monday, 18 April 2016

Before this, when you did what all parents do but never want to, when you imagined in those half-asleep moments what it is to lose a child, you thought of finality. Of a sudden void. A world that's all before and no after. Because that's the only way death makes sense to the living. As an ending. As something that ends. It's the only way a parent might prepare themselves for the worst possible event, and that's what nightmares are. Training for a race you pray you'll never run.

But it's not that. It doesn't end. There is no line drawn underneath. To lose a child is to fill the calendar of your life with dates you can't forget. The date of the death. The date of the funeral. The birthdays missed. Every year after that is a gauntlet of unhappy anniversaries. The life of the one you lost does not stop, you're forced to live it without them.

And now here's another date to add that didn't used to mean anything. Alan comes and you make tea and he tells you Morgan's body parts have been released. His brain. His blood. The samples that were taken. You can have them interred with Morgan if you like. You can suffer that trauma, or you can have them respectfully cremated, which you do, and you ask never to be told when it happens, so that a year on, and every year after, there isn't another date to reach for, to get through.

You talk to Sue and the boys and it's decided. Morgan's ashes should be scattered on the beach in Newquay where he sat with his friends and watched the sun set down behind the ocean like the slow closing of a bright eye. Where he thought of his future and was happy. You all think it's a great idea. But no one smiles.

Tuesday, 17 May 2016

The trial is almost here, which is why Detective Jason Downes is in your lounge, setting his mug down on the coffee table. Because until now there has been no use for you. The prosecution teams have been building their case, the defence teams figuring out how to defend against it. You weren't there when Morgan was murdered, so, whether you like it or not, you're superfluous to proceedings, beyond your determination to look the accused in the eye and the fact you won't have peace until you know exactly what happened that night. Until you get justice. And it's that need to know that's got you how you are right now, leaning forward, heart beating like there's a bird trapped inside your chest, as Detective Downes begins to speak.

He wants you to watch the CCTV footage.

To watch your son being murdered.

You've spoken to Olivia about this. She says sometimes it can help to understand what has happened and isn't always as bad as you imagine. You glance at Sue, see the dread she's drowning in, and you hope Olivia is right. But the look in Sue's eyes, it turns to something new then. Something tough. Something solid. Sue doesn't talk much, not at these things, not normally. But now she says, 'What about Declan Gray?'

Declan Gray. When you first heard his name and those of his co-defendants, they felt abstract. How could it be that their names would be entwined with Morgan's forever when they'd never known one another? But since the funeral, and since hearing their pleas, the urge to know more about them has been growing, or rather awakening. So you started asking people you work with and drink with. People from around town. Nuneaton people. Calling in a few favours. *Do you know anything about Declan Gray, Karlton Gray and Simon Rowbotham?* Because finding out the truth of what happened to Morgan is your only chance of rest. And knowing the truth means knowing everything.

This is what you learned: Declan Gray was convicted of manslaughter when he was fifteen, a crime for which he served just four and a half years in a young offenders' institution. Adrian Howard was thirty-eight when Declan Gray bumped into him on Black-A-Tree Road and asked him for a cigarette and, when refused, punched him and stamped on him with enough force that he died a couple of months later of a pulmonary embolism. Not only that. Declan Gray was released on licence for this offence, but recalled to prison twice, once for breaching his licence conditions and once for a suspected aggravated burglary. And despite it all, Declan Gray was released from custody on 16 June 2015, just four and a half months before he murdered Morgan.

'How has a young man like him been able to kill two people?' Sue says.

Perhaps because you can't hold back any more, you can tell when other people are hiding something. It's in a licked lip or a fluttered eyelid. It's in a clipped breath. It's in Jason, sitting on your sofa, sipping from the mug again now the tea has cooled.

'He slipped through the net,' Jason says.

He slipped through the net?

That feeling. The sense that there is more to be known. A shadow across your heart.

This isn't the first time you've had that feeling. Not the first time you've had questions for the police, either. You remember it now, when you knocked on their door, instead of them on yours.

You were getting ready for work one Sunday morning – your shift pattern having severed another relaxing weekend in two – reluctantly pulling on your boots to go drive a truck. The door opened and Morgan appeared. He was fourteen and crying. It took a second for him to catch his breath, two more for you to ask if he was OK. But he wasn't.

He'd been out riding his bike when he'd cycled straight into the lead of a man walking his dog that he hadn't seen stretched across the pavement like the tape on a finishing line. Because he'd hit the middle of the lead, the dog had been pulled sharply, and Morgan had been knocked clean off his bike and into the road. The dog was startled but fine. Morgan lay injured on the pavement, where the man stood over him, the veins in his forehead squirming and spittle bursting from his lips like sparks as he screamed abuse at a boy too shocked to allow himself to cry.

'Right,' you said, pulling on your jacket and forgetting about your job. 'Let's go find him.' You jumped straight into the car, and without thinking much about what you might do when you got there, you found the man, still not far from the street where it happened. Stopping the car a little too quickly, you bumped the kerb as you pulled up alongside him.

'Oi!' you shouted, jumping out, pointing at the man and making your voice sound deep and gravelly. The man had calmed since Morgan's retelling of events, and there, mid-Sunday morning, on a quiet residential street, he looked like any other dog owner enjoying a pleasant walk. On seeing Morgan he immediately started apologising, placing his hand on Morgan's back and saying he'd been worried about the dog, that he hadn't realised Morgan, whose cheeks were now even redder than normal, had hurt himself.

Morgan nodded, understanding that the man seemed remorseful. Perhaps he was exactly what he looked like. A middle-aged dog lover, picking up the paper to take home to his wife before putting on his slippers and making a roast dinner. But as you climbed back into the car, you heard his breathing intensify, and then him shouting as you drove away. Shouting that he was a policeman, and that first thing Monday morning he'd be putting in a report at the station. He'd be reporting Morgan for assaulting his dog.

The anger built up in you for the rest of the day, so much that you could barely concentrate on the road. He might be a policeman, but that was no excuse to be such a shit to Morgan after he'd just had an accident. It wound you up so much that you rang the police station and reported the incident to the woman who answered the phone. She was a little taken aback. This wasn't the kind of call she normally dealt with. And it certainly didn't sound like something a police officer would or should do in that situation, no way. She took your number, and that was that.

An hour later, the phone rang. It was the woman again. The caretaker – not a policeman, but the caretaker – of the police station had turned up for work and filed a complaint about Morgan. But because of you agitating, pushing, making a nuisance of yourself, it had gone horribly wrong for him, this pent-up dog walker pretending to be a police officer, and he would be disciplined for his actions. Did you want to make a formal complaint, she asked. You decided no, if he was already in trouble it would do for you. You just wanted justice, is all.

That feeling. You remember it now.

Wednesday, 18 May 2016

You must find strength where there is none.

Today is hell.

You're in a small interview room inside Nuneaton Justice Centre. There is a sofa and a coffee table, and on the wall is a small TV screen with a DVD player, but the windows are covered by blinds so no natural light gets in. No one says as much, but you guess this is where they bring vulnerable witnesses. And it stands to reason, because that's what you're about to become. A witness to your son's murder.

A detective you've not met before comes in and takes over from Alan. He's a calming presence, which is something else you've become attuned to these past few months. Something you appreciate. Imagine having his job. Imagine having this footage in your hand, knowing who you're about to show it to.

He explains to the three of you, you and Sue and Connor (who was determined to come), who are all about to be changed irreparably, that the footage you're about to see is from three angles, from three different cameras. The first is CCTV from near the flats, the second is from the NHS clinic on Pool Bank Street, and the third is from the office of a lettings agent, also on Pool Bank Street. You'll be able to watch this footage as many times as you want, but it can't be stopped or paused in any way, that's just the way it is for legal reasons. It's impossible to comprehend a desire to watch it once, let alone more, but you don't say that. You can't say anything. Your voice is deep inside you.

Are you ready?

Oh Morgan, oh no.

The boys walk across the frame. Everybody is labelled with a different colour. Shawn first, then Joe. Then Danny, Morgan, Craig and Adam. There are people running full pelt across the park towards them. One of them has his arms outstretched, like he wants this. They descend quickly, and as one of the cameras pivots away, Adam is on the ground being beaten by two men, also labelled with colours of their own. They are Declan and Karlton Gray. One of them is kicking Adam violently in the torso, the other kicking him violently in the head, which he's trying to cover with his arms as he curls up on the ground.

Declan and Karlton Gray look up, spot someone or something across the street and run towards it. Adam pulls himself to his feet, picks up his mobile phone and runs away, not yet realising that the hot liquid running down his thigh is blood from a stab wound in his buttock.

Across the street, a line of terraced houses and a wall of parked cars leave a narrow pavement between them where there is not much room to move or escape. Here, a man is attacking Craig. This is Simon Rowbotham. Shawn and

Danny and Joe have run away, but Morgan looks back and sees Craig is in trouble and – it's instinct, a split-second decision that says everything about the man he is – comes to the aid of his friend, who is being punched in the head by Rowbotham, then kicked. Craig falls forward and staggers into the street.

It's fast, the way Declan and Karlton Gray burst into shot as Morgan arrives. Morgan swings and punches the first of them, Karlton, catching him off-balance and turning him against a parked car. They grapple briefly, and Morgan is knocked to the ground. Declan appears from nowhere and hits Morgan hard in his side, towards his back. When his right hand comes up there is a blade in it. A steak knife. At no point did Morgan see Declan or the knife coming.

Karlton seems to stamp on Morgan's head as he lies there on the ground, and then tries to pull him to his feet. At the same time Declan is behind Morgan. Karlton kicks Morgan's body with a force that causes all three of them to fall backwards.

Three seconds later, Declan is standing over Morgan, who is just off-camera. The knife is still in his right hand. He stabs it down once. He stabs it down twice.

Rowbotham reappears and joins the assault on Morgan, who disappears from view for thirteen seconds before reappearing on his feet, then hitting the wing mirror of a car as he topples to the pavement. One of them kicks him. Then another.

Morgan is sitting up. There is blood on his back.

The three men beat him some more.

The glow of car headlights appears and illuminates the scene. Maybe it's the car Miroslav Holan is in, on his way to buy drinks to celebrate the arrival of his child. One of the men gestures to the other two, as if to say they should leave, which they do. They turn and walk away. They are gone.

Morgan stands. He's cowering a little as he staggers down the street for no more than ten seconds, about thirty yards or so, where he falls. He collapses on to the ground so suddenly, so hard.

Connor is furious. He's up and shouting, and the detective is trying to calm him down, but it's a losing battle. And you can't help. You can't help because you can't move. You can't do anything but ask, quietly, if you can watch it again.

Connor doesn't understand why you want to watch it again. And neither do you. But you do. So Connor is taken to another room and you watch it again. You watch it three or four times, but it's so hard to work out exactly what is going on, it all happens so quickly.

The way he staggers up the street. The way he falls to the ground.

A BAD DREAM

Morgan is walking away from you. He is wearing a blue coat with a hood so you can't see his face. He's not happy. No. He's really pissed off about something. You call him, but he will not look back at you.

Thursday, 19 May 2016

Today is your twenty-sixth wedding anniversary. The day the trial would have started, had you not requested it be put back to the start of next week because tomorrow would have been Morgan's twenty-first birthday. No matter how much you want the truth to come out, no part of you is going to let it begin just before his birthday.

You ask Sue, 'Do you want to celebrate our anniversary?' And she looks at you like you just suggested going to Mars or something. That's settled then. You don't even buy flowers. Flowers are for the grave.

Friday, 20 May 2016

He'd have had a party, there's no doubt about that. A big old party for today, his twenty-first birthday, with all his friends singing and dancing and drinking sambuca – if the landlady at the Town Talk lifted his sambuca ban for the occasion, that is, which, if he'd put his mind to it, he could have charmed her into. He'd have had the kind of party that ends like they tended to, with you getting home from a nightmare shift at 6 a.m. to find Morgan standing in the kitchen, a little worse for wear but OK, working his way through an enormous kebab, telling you that you should come to the pub with him for a drink one time, and you saying, 'Yeah right, Morgan,' before sloping off to bed and falling straight to sleep. That's the drink you never got to have with him. You'll always wish you did.

If you close your eyes, you can see him at the party. On someone's shoulders, holding up the ceiling. Your son Morgan, launching into adult life.

What would his career have been? What would his girl-friend have been like? Would they have got married? Would they have had children? Would you have had grandchildren that all looked like him? So many questions. More than he had years.

Don't. Stop it. You can't think like that.

So you do what Morgan would have wanted. You put it up on Facebook, a notice that at 6 p.m. you'll be by Morgan's grave to have a beer with him, and everyone is welcome.

When Daniel was arranging the burial, he asked if you wanted a 'three plot', and you had no idea what he meant.

'I don't get you,' you said.

'Well, you can reserve another two places.'

And you don't say it, but you think it.

What, for my other two kids?

'If you do it now, it's cheaper. For you and Sue. If you want it.'

Oh.

And you took it.

When they were lowering his coffin, you could tell what everyone was thinking. Fucking hell. How deep is that hole? Feels like it goes down forever. But there is space down there for you and Sue, if you want it.

There was a time when you considered yourself master of your own destiny. But that's slowly fading. In three or four years' time you'll view life as something you have absolutely no control over. Something that will one day just end. Whatever is going to happen is going to happen. But your plot, it's sorted, if that's where you want to end up. Maybe you will. Maybe you won't. You won't be afraid of dying, though, that's for sure. You won't be afraid of dying, because you have known death, and it can only hurt you this way once.

In the end, Sue said it best.

'I ain't being fucking buried in Nuneaton.'

Gold light dapples the cemetery through gently beckoning trees. The sky is blue and showy. The train tracks hum, a warm and constant song. But you are the only ones there.

'Oh well,' you say to Sue, clinking your glasses together to toast your son.

And then a car arrives. And then another. Then another. All arriving at the same time, as though it's scripted. And everyone who emerges throws their arms round you, until there must be twenty people – Morgan's friends, who are your friends now, and his colleagues, who are your friends now too. Joe puts music on his phone, and you say something, and you cry and you all drink a toast to Morgan with your glasses in the air, where he is, all around you.

Saturday, 21 May 2016

It wasn't your idea (Sue would say the best ones seldom are). It was Ele's idea. Ele had been Morgan's girlfriend in school, and she'd been in contact with the graffiti boys – Dave, Craig, Kyle, Trey and Danny – to see if they could paint a mural for Morgan's twenty-first birthday. They thought it was a great idea, and contacted the Urban Arts Clinic, for which Morgan had done some community work in the past, making art of his own at local festivals and painting the walls of a Nuneaton subway in memory of a girl who had tragically lost her life. The council gave funding for the paint, and, more importantly, permission to use the big wall down on Dugdale Street behind the Ropewalk Shopping Centre, so that no one who walked by – which in Nuneaton is pretty much everyone – would be able to miss it.

It was a year or two ago now that Morgan told you about the skate park down in Stockingford Recreation Ground – the Rec as it's known – about the huge blank wall that divides the ramps through the middle. Nuneaton wasn't immune to the rising rates of knife crime nationally, so he and Craig had been asked to come up with an anti-knife slogan for it, and he couldn't think of one that might strike the balance of urgency and poignancy needed to make people pay attention. EVIL THUGS STABBED ANTI-KNIFE CAMPAIGNER TO DEATH IN UNPROVOKED ATTACK might have done it. But that was just a headline written about Morgan in the *Daily Mirror* years later. Eventually they settled on a slogan and painted it in vivid orange and metallic greens, these giant letters that seemed to dance wildly along the surface, as though the words, like those who needed to read them, were on the verge of losing control.

SAVE A LIFE, LOSE A KNIFE

Morgan was pretty dismissive of his handiwork. He knew that for decades, long before the skate park even existed, the Rec had been a nesting ground for groups of bored teenagers with nowhere to be and no one who wanted them home. It was a great place to wait for trouble, or to make it if it didn't come. It was a fine spot for young men with nothing to do but fight. Somewhere to take a knife, and feel stronger, harder, safer, more important, tougher, scarier, more like a man. A place to take aggression and have it tested. Was the slogan for them, Morgan wondered? And would they pay attention if it was?

You arrive around midday, a little tender from the night before, to find a hive of activity around the wall. Loud music is playing and for a second you want to retreat. But you don't. You stand and watch Morgan's friends writing his name, each in their own style, and one, the best artist of the lot –

his tag is N4T4 – painting Morgan's portrait in the middle. His face, and the smile it's built around, slowly coming into being. And it's beautiful. A crowd of strangers have gathered, filming on their phones. And that's beautiful too, isn't it, to have no one looking at you. To have them looking at him, where he will be forever. Because Morgan is what everything you'll do from now on is all about.

And you vow that, starting Monday, you will get him the justice he deserves.

Monday, 23 May 2016

It was Olivia's idea and you do as she suggested, pack a little picnic in a cool bag. Slicing bread. Spreading butter. Cutting cheese. Everything is so banal, the morning of the trial of the men accused of your son's murder.

Alan picks you, Sue, Connor and Eamon up in a Volvo four-wheel drive for the journey to court, and it's just as well. Who knows what state you'll be in to drive back. The boys look apprehensive as Alan warns you there could be press outside. He advises you to keep your heads down and get into the courthouse as quickly as possible. But when you arrive there is no one there, and you can't be sure if you're relieved or angry. Maybe it's just another stabbing of another young man. Though it sure doesn't feel like that to you.

You're taken to a new waiting room, bigger than any you've been in before. This will be your room for the entirety of the trial. There are windows, which is a bonus, a small sofa, a low coffee table, with tea, coffee and biscuits. Who knows, when this is all over, maybe you'll never touch another biscuit again. A volunteer greets you warmly, makes sure you've got everything you need, and for a second you feel an appreciation for a stranger's kindness so intense you want to throw your arms round her.

Andrew Smith QC comes in. He's leading the prosecution for the Crown Prosecution Service, and he's immediately likeable. You weren't sure what you were expecting, but now you realise. This isn't your trial. You're not in control. The CPS are in charge, and you're nothing but an observer, which is all right, you suppose, as long as everyone gets the fate they deserve. He sits and looks you in the eyes with a steely confidence and tells you they're going for the murder charge for all three of them. That's the goal. And the evidence is strong: a triple whammy of CCTV footage, forensics and witness statements that, on the surface at least, seem undeniable. Declan Gray pleaded not guilty to murder but guilty to manslaughter, like he did the last time he killed someone. This is most likely his way of getting his sentence reduced, almost like hedging his bets. If he gets it right, he will be out in a few years, just like last time. If he gets it wrong, the manslaughter charge is the best outcome he can achieve. The other two, Karlton Gray and Simon Rowbotham, pleaded not guilty to all charges. They're probably hoping Declan will take the rap for all of it, because he's the one in the footage with the steak knife in his hand. He's the one who plunged it into your son.

Andrew leans forward, somehow even more serious than before. There is something else he needs to let you know, something important, something hard to hear.

'The defence will have their own take on events, which might include blaming Morgan's death on the medical treatment he received,' he says. 'We will see.'

The public gallery, high up above the courtroom, is packed with your extended family, Morgan's aunts, uncles and cousins. You wanted them here. To surround you with support.

To be the home team. But you realise you're sitting at the back. It's Alan who makes people move so you, Sue, Connor and Eamon can sit at the front, which you're grateful for. And when you do, the courtroom sprawls beneath you, like the view of the stage from the circle in a theatre. It is filling with barristers and clerks as though bustling with insects, and the defendants shuffling nervously to their seats, Simon in a scruffy suit and tie sitting behind the two brothers, Declan and Karlton. None of them speak. It's as though they've never met. As though they're not all accused of killing the same man.

The jury enter through a side door. Finally, in comes Judge Griffith-Jones, in his thick, dusty cobweb of a wig, to start the proceedings in which you've no choice but to place your faith.

You hold Sue's hand.

This is really happening, love.

Your eyes fall on the defendants as the CCTV of Morgan's final moments is played to the court. Declan, the older brother, leans forward, watching the screen like a hawk, not just with his eyes but with his whole squat, boxy frame, as though analysing every angle, every beat for proof of his non-existence.

Of no chase through an empty park.

Of no blade glinting in his hand.

Of no Morgan on the pavement.

And for a second, just a second, you and Declan Gray want exactly the same thing. A film of an event that never happened, and Morgan by your side, watching nothing take place.

Karlton, the younger brother, reacts differently. He slides downwards in his seat like a sulky teenager, as though refusing to acknowledge the screen is even there. Simon meanwhile keeps perfectly still, like he's hoping that, if he does not move, all this shall pass, this blip in space time that has landed him somewhere he ought not to be, this freak cosmic mistake. But this is really happening. You're all learning that together.

And as Andrew gives his opening statement, you're all learning this too:

Morgan died from stab wounds to the chest, heart and left lung. This wound would have been fatal.

Look at their faces.

He had a stab wound to his back and left shoulder.

Do they hear it?

He had a fractured nose and left eye socket.

Do you hear it?

He suffered a brain injury, probably from the stamping and the kicking.

Do you see what it is that you did?

Right now, you need to remember: there are good people out there too. You need to remember, these aren't the men whose hands were last on your son. What about the air-ambulance doctor who tried to save Morgan's life on the street? Don't forget him. Don't forget that when he arrived at the scene, Morgan had stopped breathing. He opened up Morgan's chest, because the knife had pierced Morgan's left ventricle, and Morgan's heart was pumping out blood into the sac that surrounded it. As Morgan walked up the street after the attack, the blood compressed his heart, causing him to black out and fall to the pavement. The doctor cut open the sac to release the blood, then massaged Morgan's heart by hand to restart it. And he did. This man brought Morgan back to life. He gave him a chance. Morgan felt the hands of good people last.

You're all learning this too:

After Declan and Karlton were arrested they were taken to a police station where officers overheard a conversation they shared through the walls of a cell. And as Andrew reads it out in his opening statement to the court, you take out a pen and a notepad, and you write it down so it reads like a scene from a play:

DECLAN: Yo.
KARLTON: What?
DECLAN: We're fucked man.
KARLTON: Why?
DECLAN: I've seen the CCTV and Danielle is
            talking.
KARLTON: What's she said?
DECLAN: We're fucked and we're going to jail.
KARLTON: What's it showing?
DECLAN: The camera shows everything man.
KARLTON: I'm not staying in here, I'm going to top
            myself man.
DECLAN: I'm going down for twenty years at least for
            this.
KARLTON: How long will I get?
DECLAN: At least ten years.
KARLTON: I can't do prison.
DECLAN: One moment of madness and we're all
            fucked.

They talk a lot. They all talk a lot. But when they're interviewed by police, they have no comments to make about anything at all.

AN INCOMPLETE LIST OF WAYS TO BETTER PREPARE FOR THE TRIAL OF YOUR CHILD'S KILLERS

Practical:
Eat toast first thing.
Always take a packed lunch.
Write everything down.

Impractical:
Know you'll be made to wait.
Know you'll be disappointed.
Know you'll be angry.

Tuesday, 24 May 2016

You look down at the defendants' seats. At the seats of the jurors. All empty, like a bad opening night. All that time you've spent trying to prepare yourself for waiting, disappointment and anger, and when it comes down to it, you really weren't prepared at all.

Day two of the trial, and the defendants have refused to leave the prison to come to court, Andrew says. They didn't get a hot meal or a shower when they got back last night, and so, well, they're protesting. The defendants – *stab wound, chest, heart, left lung, fractured nose, eye socket, brain injury* – are protesting their treatment. They won't be coming to court today. You want to hear how your scream echoes in a courtroom. How loud it is, if it gets trapped in the high ceiling. But you don't.

'We will postpone court today,' the judge says, with his posh voice from his high seat. 'But you can tell them that I will not be able to do this again. We will go on without them next time. I don't want them not to have a fair trial, so tell them.'

And just like that, your day is done.

Thursday, 26 May 2016

All of Morgan's friends who were there that night spoke before the court yesterday: Craig, Adam, Joe, Shawn and Danny. They were all cross-examined, all asked how drunk they were on a scale of one to ten, and whether they shouted back when they were heckled with racist abuse from the balcony, as though in some way they incited what was to follow. As if Morgan's murder was in some way their fault. Maybe it was as hard for them to relive it as it was for you to hear, and you'll never know – some of them, for their own reasons, find it difficult to talk to you and always will. But this is different.

The young woman shuffles in her seat, and you realise it's the first time you've heard anyone you don't know describe what happened that night. Until Danielle, Karlton's now ex-girlfriend, appears on screen in a pre-recorded interview given after the arrests, you've not heard Morgan's last moments in the words of someone he didn't know. Someone who was there.

'Me and Karlton were in the kitchen and we heard Dec come in, and he said, "Get the fuck outside Karlton, or I'll smash your head in."'

Declan was really drunk, she says. He had a bottle of vodka in his hand and had been on drugs for days. Karlton was scared of his older brother Declan and easily influenced by him. He and Danielle followed Declan back out to the balcony, where they saw Morgan walking away through the park with his friends.

'Dec and them were going mad, saying, "Come on then." Si said, "Let's go and do them." They went down. I went down because I didn't want Karlton to fight and I wanted to pull him away. We got to Pool Bank Street and Karlton has ran over to one of them, and them two are having a fight, and Dec has run over to one of them.'

She moves her fist back and forth, as though forcing a saw through wood.

'Dec was doing this. I thought he was just punching him. Then in the background you can see Si kicking the fuck out of this other lad, and Karlton has punched him in the face. Dec has come running over again, and all of them are on top of this lad. His mates have run off. You can see Si get this belt and put it round his neck, strangling him. I thought they were just having a fight . . . Dec has then come running over and said, "I've just stabbed that lad." Karlton asked what he did with the knife. He said, "I've chucked it over there." He seemed worried, really, really worried.'

Asked if she knew Declan Gray carried a knife, she says: 'No, Dec can fight on his own. He don't need no weapon. I was like, "What sort of knife was it?" and he said it was just a steak knife.'

But in court, things change. You lean forward on the balcony, focusing on the quiet, nervous trill of Danielle's voice, and her eyes that saw Morgan that night, as she's questioned by Karlton's QC. Danielle now says she 'did not really see what happened', and that during the filmed interview she was 'basically telling them what I had seen on camera', having already been shown a CCTV recording of the incident by the police. He puts to her:

'At the beginning, when Karlton started to get involved, you handed a knife to Declan Gray.'

'No,' she says.

Declan's QC puts it to Danielle that, a few weeks after the murder, she had a conversation on WhatsApp in which she discussed her worry that Declan would grass her up about handing him the knife when he ran out of the flat. She denies ever saying that. She denies having WhatsApp at all.

You sit and you listen and you realise. Like a beam of light refracting through a prism, Morgan's story has become a thousand different stories. A thousand different perspectives on the same terrible truth. Some are born of grief. Some of anger. Some of fear. Some of self-preservation. Some of love. Some of the dark desire people have to make themselves a part of the story, or move closer to the centre. Some to be nearer to Morgan in death, some to be further away. Some to deal with loss, some to build their role in it. They manifest in Facebook posts, or drunken conversations, or public art projects with money raised in Morgan's name about which you know nothing. They manifest in witness statements, pleas and denials. In court testimony. In hearsay. In below-the-line comments, and gossip in shops. And you will want to control them, these versions of your pain, but you will learn that you can't. Not always. There are a thousand different stories about the taking of your son, and sometimes you can only sit and listen.

Here's another.

In the afternoon a brain trauma expert appears via video link from London. The defence team interview him about how Morgan's brain trauma was caused. Whether there was a chance that it was not the result of a kick or a punch or a stamp, but could in fact have been caused by him falling over, as though Morgan's death was a result of him throwing himself to the ground. Under cross-examination, the expert talks about how trauma can cause concussion, which would lead to dizziness, and the inability to defend oneself. A little like a punch-drunk boxer, unable to raise his arms and parry jabs or throw a hook. Morgan had no defence wounds, according to the pathologist, meaning it is possible that the brain trauma had already happened before Declan, Karlton and Simon punched him and kicked him and stamped on his head.

You see what they are doing. The doubt they are introducing. The angle they've found to save themselves. Another version. Another story. Another beam of light from the prism. Another layer to your pain. And when they're done you take your family's hands, and you guide them outside into the sun.

Behind the court, Jephson Gardens curl around the River Leam like a lover. The sky is clear, the clouds are plump. On days like this you can lie back on the grass, eat your sandwiches and watch the gold light bounce off a quaint greenhouse, or fall in stripes across the lake as ducks discuss the dogfights of butterflies. It can feel like an entirely different world.

Wednesday, 1 June 2016

You see it most days, seared inside your eyelids when you close them. That image of Morgan, staggering down the road, then hitting the floor, like he's been dropped from height. You see it in the mirror when you brush your teeth. You see it from the window of Alan's car on the way to court. You see it now, and every time you look at Declan, Karlton and Simon, who laugh and joke among themselves when the jury isn't sitting. Who barely glance at the documents that detail the evidence against them. Who never look back up at you.

You see it now.

But what do they see – Declan, Karlton and Simon – as a forensic scientist takes the stand and tells the court that Morgan's DNA was found on a black puffa jacket in a Meadow Court flat used by the defendants?

And not just that, but a pair of Adidas trainers, with all twenty points of Declan's DNA on them, and inside the tongue Morgan's blood.

Oh, and a steak knife, discarded close to the scene and yet somehow only discovered days later, with all the components of Morgan's DNA found on the blade, and Declan's the most prominent DNA on the handle.

Do they see light slipping away? Or do they peer into the darkness and still see sun?

Tuesday, 7 June 2016

When Andrew comes into the waiting room you're half expecting to be sent home again. That's what happened last Friday, and last Monday too. You were dragged all the way here for nothing but free coffee and talk of legal arguments. You're not even sure what a legal argument is, but it must have been a bloody big one to suck two whole days out of the trial. If Andrew sits down and tells you there are more legal arguments today, you might ask if this is going to go on long enough for you to retrain as a solicitor and join in.

But that's not what he tells you. Instead, he tells you why court was really called off.

On Friday Declan smuggled a razor blade into court in his mouth.

'He did what?' you say. But you've heard nothing until you've heard this.

On Monday Karlton smuggled a weapon into court up his anus. Yep. That meant both days they had to suspend and search the court to keep everyone safe.

'They're playing silly games and the judge is not going to be happy about it,' Andrew says.

'Good,' you say, 'because I'm beginning to think this trial is being led from the dock.'

'I can assure you, Mr Hehir,' he says, 'that is not the case.'

The more you think about it, the angrier you become, so angry that the shrapnel of your thoughts pocks your face. You pace the waiting room and your family know better than to approach.

The jury won't be told what Declan and Karlton did, and they know that. It's a huge open secret and they're entitled to it. They're still young men and they already understand how to play the justice system at chess. What will happen at the end? Will they lay down the queen, or kick the board up in the air when they lose?

Back in court, you peer over the balcony to see Declan and Karlton handcuffed to guards.

'For the safety of the court,' Alan says.

And you don't enjoy it, it doesn't make you happy, and it doesn't help you because nothing can.

But it's important, Colin, that you know this. When they were arrested, they were scared, and they lied, and they turned on each other. Maybe they did see their futures disintegrate, just like yours, even if they couldn't comprehend what it meant.

*

A series of witnesses take to the stand, and as each of them testifies you're able to build a fuller picture of what happened in the hours after Morgan was attacked. On 1 November at 4.40 a.m., seven hours after Morgan had been stabbed and forty-five minutes after he died in hospital, a police dog handler was searching the area around the flats, not far from the crime scene. He noticed three figures in a doorway, two men and a woman. The officer told them to stand still, but the two men ran, leaving the woman, Danielle, alone. The officer pursued the men, catching one, who even in the dark was pale and sweaty-looking. He was in a garden area, by a gate.

'What's your name mate?' the officer said, tightening the leash.

'Declan,' the man said, which was just as the officer assumed.

'You're under arrest.'

'What's all this about?'

'I am arresting you on suspicion of murder.'

Down at the station, toxicology results showed that Declan had in his body alcohol, cannabis, cocaine and a ringworm treatment the cocaine had been cut with. In the time between the murder and his arrest, he'd been in a car to Coventry with Karlton and Danielle to score crack. He was interviewed under caution but gave no comment.

Simon was arrested later and, understandably, wanted to know exactly what for. Murder, they told him.

'That's a bit of a fucking charge!' he said. 'It was Declan Gray! I wasn't there, but I can tell you where the knife is!'

Karlton was arrested later still. His eyes filled with tears as they showed him the CCTV footage in an interview room, the interviewing officer saying Morgan's name while he watched.

'If only I knew about the knife,' he said. And then, about his brother Declan, 'I don't give a shit mate, he's a fucking prick mate. If I'd known about the knife I'd have given him a rugby tackle. I feel so shitty, really horrible, I didn't know about the knife, it wouldn't have ended up like that, there was three of us on him, it should have just been a fight.'

When you get home it's still warm. You change out of your smart clothes into shorts and T-shirts, open a few beers and sit on the outdoor sofa Sue bought for exactly this kind of evening. You remember the look on Declan's face, how furious he was with Karlton, who was sinking into his seat as the police officer read aloud what he'd said in his interview after he was arrested. The two of them sat together, handcuffed to prison guards, refusing to look at one another. Stitching his own brother up like a kipper.

You lean over to Connor and Eamon and clink their glasses. These young men, who'll always need each other now, who'll always rely on each other, stand up for each other, be there for each other. These brothers, these fine, upstanding young men.

Thursday, 9 June 2016

The only surprise is that it took so long. He should have said it from the very beginning. It shouldn't have taken CCTV, forensics, witnesses to the crime and the mouth on his brother.

'Declan Gray has changed his plea to guilty to murder.'

When Andrew says the words they mean nothing to you. It should be a resolution. But it's not. Not until you know everything.

'What happens now?' you say, trying hard to concentrate on Andrew's explanation. While it's good that Declan has changed his plea, it opens up a set of new problems. The law has it that evidence involving Declan can now not be used in the cases against Karlton and Simon, to ensure they have a fair trial. The prosecution are therefore hoping Karlton and Simon will plead guilty to manslaughter. That's what they're going for. The goalposts have moved. And it feels like they're getting away with it.

What it doesn't feel like is justice. You throw your hands up in anger. Why guilty to manslaughter? Why not guilty to murder? They were all there. They all attacked him. It's all on fucking film! 'I'm not a gambling man,' you say, 'but just put it to the jury. They've seen the CCTV. Let them decide if it's murder or manslaughter.'

But they can't do that, Andrew says. It's been decided already, without you. They don't want to risk Karlton and Simon walking free from court. So they're going to push for them to plead guilty to a charge of manslaughter. That's how this is going to work. There is no consideration for the want of the family or the victim. This is about the defendants vs the CPS, not about Morgan, and it has been all along.

You sit in the waiting room, utterly deflated, while just a few metres away Simon's girlfriend and Karlton's mother are in the courtroom trying to persuade them to plead guilty to manslaughter, like they've been told. To not risk a murder conviction and a longer sentence – these men, who were punching and kicking and stamping on Morgan in the moments before he died. A courtroom you're not allowed into.

Friday, 10 June 2016

It works. Simon Rowbotham and Karlton Gray change their pleas to guilty of the lesser charge of manslaughter. There is no longer any guilt or innocence for the jury to deliberate. All that remains is for the judge to pass down his sentence. As far as you're concerned they've got away with murder.

Andrew meets you in the waiting room. It's difficult to know whose anger he senses, yours or Sue's, but you don't have to speak for him to know it.

'How many years are they going to get?' you say.

'I can't tell you,' he says. 'That's up to the judge.'

You bristle as you look him in the eye.

'Then we want to sit in the court, for the sentencing.'

He umms and ahhs.

'That's going to be difficult,' he says. And you don't say anything, so he has to keep talking. 'But we will see if we can make room ... Anyway, about your Victim Personal Statement. Can I incorporate it in my closing speech? It will make it a little tidier.'

Tidier?

And then you hit him with it.

'If we can sit in the court, yes.'

He's taken aback by that. By you not taking anything other than yes for an answer. And he has to agree, doesn't he? So you will sit in the court. Finally, you will look into their eyes.

Saturday, 11 June 2016

You float above the garden with the pollen. This is supposed to be a celebration. The trial is over. They were found guilty. Below, the pinkening heads of Morgan's friends, pulling chilled beer bottles from a tub of ice and triumphantly holding them aloft like new babies. Smoke from the barbecue rises up around you, but you don't feel anything. This doesn't feel like justice so you don't feel you can rest.

Down in the corner, Sue is alone. You want to get to her, but can't, and the heat carries you over the fences and the neighbours' gardens, over the trees and the roofs and the chimneys, over the town that once knew you as you knew it, further and further away.

Monday, 13 June 2016

The court looks different from down here. You're over to one side of the judge, about three feet below him. You can hear the rustle of his wig, the tight percussion of his breath, smell the tang of wood polish and nervous sweat, see the eyes that widen as they turn in the light to catch yours.

Five feet to your right is your old solicitor. The one who helped sell your business. The one who helped buy your house. The one who knew your family. He does not look at you. Perhaps he can't. Good.

Up in the gallery, a line of friendly faces conjure smiles from nothing. Your brother Dave and sister Geraldine. Your nieces, Emma and Joanne. Your mother, who raises her hand and waves because she so wants to hold you – her son – but she can't.

The jury file into their seats and it is time.

Declan Gray, Karlton Gray and Simon Rowbotham stand like soldiers on the wrong side's army. And you? You do what deep down you've known you'd do since the moment you found out Morgan was murdered. You stare into their eyes. Through these metres of air, this lifetime of pain they have given you. You want to see them. You want them to see you. To see the bending of you, the ways you have warped. You want them to feel it. To see if they feel at all. All these other people in the court may think you're being brave, but bravery is not what this is. You're not brave. You're bereft. You don't want revenge. You want remorse.

Simon Rowbotham looks straight ahead. His face is gaunt and blank, not twisted into a grin as it once was on television, guiding a camera crew around the estate he claimed to run. It is hollow.

The court hears that Simon was taken into care at seventeen months old. He has 105 previous convictions going back to 1990, including instances of robbery and assault. And the judge speaks.

Simon Valentine Rowbotham is sentenced to eight years in prison for the manslaughter of Morgan Hehir.

Karlton Gray twists and fidgets, his restless eyes zipping around the courtroom like bluebottles until he spots you, staring back at him. And through the nerves and the tension, his instinct kicks in. He stares back, as though he wants to fight, to leap over the dock, through a wall of clerks, and stop you with his boots and fists. Not for one second do you stop staring back.

The court hears that Karlton has ADHD and learning difficulties, is under the malign influence of his older brother Declan, and that he lived with his mother until he was nine, whereupon he was taken into the care of his grandfather. The court hears he has twenty-two previous convictions, two of which were related to actual bodily harm. And the judge speaks.

Karlton Mark Gray is sentenced to six years and nine months in prison for the manslaughter of Morgan Hehir.

Declan Gray won't look at you. He will never look at you.

And the judge speaks. He tells the court:

'This ferocious and vicious attack took place between groups of people. It was totally unjustifiable and must have the appropriate sentence when someone loses their life. The terrible feature of the attack is that Declan Gray entered it with a vicious-looking steak knife with intent of using it to cause serious injury to any man in the group that you could get your hands on.'

And then,

'I have watched the footage more than once and I am not sure you intended to kill, as when the very vulnerable Morgan got up to get away you did not carry on at that point.'

Declan Jay Gray is sentenced to life for the murder of Morgan Hehir, and must serve twenty-three years and nine months in prison before being considered for parole.

Those words.

I am not sure you intended to kill.

You're shaking your head and you can tell Sue is as furious as you are, because this, this isn't justice. Eight years and six years for the manslaughter of your son? An allowance made for the fact that Morgan stood up and tried to walk away after he was stabbed, and that they let him, until he collapsed? With sentencing discounts, all three of them, just for pleading guilty in the face of overwhelming evidence?

I am not sure you intended to kill.

You look up at the judge, who you realise is looking down at you, at the redness of your face, the fury. And he's talking to you. 'Remember the good times . . . and try to stay together as a family.'

And there you were, thinking he was going to apologise for the way the court has handled these men, these men who smuggled weapons into the sanctity of this room just to derail the process the judge represents. Here he is, not even extending his sympathy to your family who have lost everything. You want to leap out of your seat, point your finger at this silly man in his stupid wig and dress who knows nothing of your sorrow and how it's just been deepened, and tell him to go fuck himself. But you don't. Because you'd be leaving this courtroom through the wrong doors. You'd probably go to prison for a decade. Longer than you'd get for the manslaughter of your son. So you swallow it all. What else are you meant to do? You're a good man. You keep your mouth shut though your heart is broken open.

Back in the waiting area you're surrounded by your friends and family, and everything is shifting around you in ways you don't understand. Andrew says they'll appeal to the Attorney General that the sentences are too lenient, but Sue is having none of it. She tears a leaflet from the wall and slams it down on the table. In the last few weeks of waiting, she's read it front to back over and over again.

'It says in there that if the case goes before a jury it's the judge's decision if any discount is given. He didn't have to give it!'

'Yes,' Andrew says, seeing your anger welling in the dents made by your fingers on the seats. 'But the jury didn't have to make a judgment, so it counts as an early plea.' That's total shit to your ears. You hold Sue but your arms feel heavy.

The police ask if you have a statement prepared, like they asked for. And you have. You've done your homework. And maybe you were foolish, because when you were writing the words you wanted read on the steps of the court, with a hundred microphones jostling for position at the mouth of a spokesperson, with you standing behind them defiant, you'd imagined it as a moment of triumph in darkness, like the kind you've seen on TV. You'd read them back to yourself, envisioning it as a kind of victory speech, a welcome comma in your suffering. You'd pictured the television news cameras panning over the faces of your family, not smiling, in pain, but content that justice had been served.

But no.

You take the piece of paper from your inside jacket pocket, unfold it and strike out all the stuff about being happy with the sentences handed down by the judge to Karlton and Simon. In its place you write more about Morgan. About who he was. You want everyone to know he was good. Not like them. Not like those fucking bastards who killed him. And you read it back, silently mouthing the words that taste like salt.

'Morgan should be here today. He was living his life to the full and doing the things he loved. Music, art, and watching Nuneaton Boro at the weekend after working all week at the George Eliot Hospital. He was out having a few beers with his friends on a night out in the town. Declan Gray, Karlton Gray and Simon Rowbotham changed everything in our lives, never to be the same again. With the help of friends and family we have managed to get through these dark times. We welcome the sentence of life in prison for Declan Gray, but feel our life sentence has already began of life without Morgan.'

'Do you want to talk to the press?' someone asks. For a second you consider it, but a sideways look from Sue confirms what you already know. You're too mad to be in control. You might say something you regret, and your family don't deserve to have their good reputation tarnished by you unloading on some unsuspecting journalist with a microphone.

So you pack up your things, put your arms round the boys and you leave, content you'll never see the inside of this room again. But when you step outside, it's not to the rapid-fire popping of flashbulbs or a chorus of reporters' voices asking you for comment. There are no television cameras, no broadcast satellites on vans. There is no one asking questions, and so no answers to give.

That's when it hits you. To the world, to everyone outside your bubble of loss, Morgan was just another young man killed on a night out. When the rumours that ripped through the town ran out of steam, he became nothing more than a statistic. A number on a knife-crime spreadsheet and a face painted on a wall.

Ask yourself, did you do something wrong? You played ball all along, never speaking to the press because that's exactly what the police told you to do. And then you beat yourself up. You weren't box office. You were dry, you were boring. There is no outcry about the sentences, and that's your fault for not speaking out. You didn't even kick up a fuss to get the CCTV footage shown on the news. How can you expect to have stoked the public's righteous indignation if they never even knew the facts of the case? What if all you've done is make the CPS look good? Let them tick the little box next to successful prosecution without taking a risk or a chance in your name. Handed them a win.

You have to ask yourself, when push comes to shove, did you do everything you could?

You have to ask yourself, what can you do now?

You have to ask yourself, how can there be justice, until you know the truth?

Truth

Tuesday, 14 June 2016

You stay up late because you can't fall asleep. Every time you try, your eyes burn. They want to see everything. You Google the name of Judge Griffith-Jones, because you can't stop hearing the same words over and over.

I am not sure you intended to kill.
I am not sure you intended to kill
I am not sure you intended to kill.

And you realise where you've seen his name before. Judge Griffith-Jones. He's the same judge who sentenced Declan Gray for his manslaughter conviction in 2010. When he stamped on an innocent man's head. When he kicked Adrian Howard so hard that he died two months later from a pulmonary embolism. He's the same judge who sentenced Declan Gray for that crime to four and a half years in a young offenders' institution, saying as he sent him down that he had a 'lack of intent' to cause serious harm.

When you do fall asleep, it's because you can't go on thinking about how, if he'd received a longer sentence then, maybe he'd have still been in prison, and not free to murder Morgan. Your body stops you, shuts you down, a mercy you find nowhere else.

They haunt you though, these words:

He slipped through the net.

Declan Gray slipped through the net.

And until you understand what they mean, they always will.

Thursday, 16 June 2016

Morgan's friend Joe rolls the stainless-steel drum of the washing machine down on to the sand. Eamon and Craig pack the hollow beneath it with charcoal. You lay burgers across the centre, frame them with plump sausages and tooth-white halloumi. Sue watches the flame roll upwards, and as the metal heats the meat begins to sizzle.

You're more rested than yesterday, after the long drive from Nuneaton to Newquay. Joe and Millie gave you their bed, which was an extraordinary kindness, and now you're able to recline on Little Fistral beach, plucking open the ring pull on a beer and letting sea air knead out the scent of sunned skin. There is no one else here. You lie back in wait for the golden hour, Sue by your side, light edging slowly down her face.

There is a part of your pain reserved for the fact that you can't really talk to her any more. Not because she isn't there or won't listen, but because maybe she's having a good day, and you don't want to bring her down.

Instead you've been confiding in Olivia, for hour after hour, telling her of your fears and insecurities about what will become of your family now. It never occurred to you that you might be a therapy kind of a guy, but it helps and these days you enjoy it. Her reassurances lift the mist, and even though you know it will descend again, you can appreciate the bits in between. A lot of the time you just want her advice. Whatever part of your mind you used to rely on for sound judgement is crushed beneath sorrow. You're not that guy any more, good old Colin with his head screwed on. You're Colin with his head screwed off. That's what they'll know you as now.

You've been showing Olivia the letters sent home from Eamon's school about his attendance, which has dropped below 92 per cent. There were numerous meetings with his teachers when you tried your best to explain that you only care about him attending for the social side of things. To be with his friends. To make him feel better. He's endured too much for one so young, and no matter how good he is, no matter how brave he is, no matter you've enough pride in him to fill a cosmos, he needs help just the same. They acknowledge your words, but come back with targets the government have set for attendance, and remind you that his exams are next year. There isn't a next year, don't they see that? There is nothing other than now for you and your family. So you need Olivia to ease your anxiety. To remind you that, in time, everything will be OK, shit but OK, even if you don't believe it.

You stand and walk down the beach towards the sunset. Craig tells you all about how, when he'd been here with Morgan, they swam in the ocean at the end of the day and drove home in their soaking-wet clothes. The others join you where the sea kisses the sand.

You didn't prepare what to say. How could you?

'This was Morgan's happy place. There is a little bit of him here now.'

You open the jar and let him go. The waves come as they must, and as they take him they wash up old memories around your feet.

Out in Connemara, the mossy rocks of the headland stand defiant against the Atlantic, as though guarding the earth from a war in the water. But that day it was still. You, Morgan and Connor chose a fine one to sit there with fishing rods, dangling lines through the mirror of the sun. The wait was long, but with your boys beside you time became a gift. As the day wound to a close and your bellies started to rumble, you readied the kids, just teenagers then, to pack away their kit. Time to head back, luckless.

But, right at the last possible moment, there was a tug on Morgan's line and his lips split to a smile. You stood together and slowly reeled it in. The fish was small, but the glory eclipsed it. Morgan held his catch above his head and danced a victory jig. He had conquered the part of the world where he was, in the short time that he had.

Wednesday, 6 July 2016

Here you are. Woah, check you out. You're doing OK! You're out of bed, and pulling on your uniform, and making your sandwiches, and watching some crap on daytime television because you have a little time before you need to leave. You're kind of enjoying it in a way you're not totally willing to admit, but that's all right because Sue is at work, Eamon is at school and Connor is at the gym, and what they don't know they can't take the piss out of you for. You're doing that kind of OK.

That's when Alan comes for the last time. He hands you a small package, explaining how well it's been cleaned up. How remarkable it is, the attention to detail when removing all the dirt and the blood.

He hands you Morgan's watch.

Everyone knows this about losing a child. It'll hit you. It'll always catch you up. You'll think you're dealing with it, and then WHAM, when you least expect it, the grief comes and cuts you down like long grass. All you can hope is that you're not out in public, or alone, or behind the wheel of a truck. What you hope for has shifted so far.

But you're never prepared for what triggers it. It's different for everybody. For some, maybe it's photographs. To be confronted with a face that can't be touched. But for you, photographs remind you of all the times you held him. Maybe it's tastes or smells, a fresh-baked buttered croissant or an iced bun so sweet it pricks the tongue like the ones they used to enjoy. But for you they keep him here, they don't remind you that he's gone. Maybe it's the fullness of a pillow not slept on, an unworn shirt or an empty plate. Maybe it's a field they used to run across. A favourite cartoon. A phrase that sounded better in the mouth of someone who won't say it again. Maybe it's the way an i is dotted, or the way a t is crossed. The leaving open of a door you used to want closed. The creak of a floorboard that used to be stepped over. Maybe it's just the feel of the breeze.

For you it's Morgan's watch, because you realise: this is it. This is all that came home from that night out. Not his clothes or his shoes or his phone or his wallet. And not him. Just this, his watch, which ceaselessly counts the time since it was last round his wrist. You fall to the ground and weep with a sadness so whole it feels like the completion of a pain only hinted at before. It weakens and hollows you. Makes you brittle, crushes you. Loses what's left to the wind.

'What is grieving?' you say to Olivia. She's unshakeable usually, but there's movement now, a flicker in her eye.

'It's what you are doing,' she says. 'It's you missing him.'

You don't make it in to work that day or the days after. The house fills back up again and, like the time on the watch, you tick on.

Thursday, 28 July 2016

The commitment of some companies to their hold music being shit is astonishing, isn't it? Is it actually designed to make people give up on waiting? Because if it is, it might just work this time. This – sitting on the arm of the sofa with the phone pressed against your ear listening to some of the worst music ever committed to record – has quite possibly been the single most boring twenty minutes of your life. And considering you're a man who spends most of his time stuck in traffic, that's saying something.

You know you should be moving forward. Finding some version of peace, now that the people who killed Morgan are locked up in prison cells. But the reality is there's no moving forward until every wrinkle is flattened. And sometimes, when you flatten a wrinkle, an even bigger one pops up in its place.

'Hello,' a man says at last, 'you're through to Apple, how can I help?' and you feel like crying with gratitude just to hear a human voice. Now all you have to do is find the words to explain your problem in a way that doesn't shock him into silence, or immediately get you put back on hold. And frankly, 'It all began when my son was murdered . . .' probably isn't it. Except, it is.

Morgan's MacBook barely ever left his side. He spent his first decent pay cheque on it. It's where he kept all his photos and videos of his graffiti artwork. It's where he recorded all the music he wrote and performed.

Inside it are the contents of his mind, and it's that which you and Sue miss most. You'd handed it to the police not long after the arrests in case it somehow held clues they could pluck from the cloud, but to your shock they handed it back a few months later, saying it was too expensive for them to unlock – their budget wouldn't allow it – and Apple were notoriously difficult to deal with. How much was too much to investigate Morgan's murder? What price the art your son left behind?

The young man on the phone is helpful. He sets you little tasks. Asks you to hold down various combinations of buttons. To relay back to him what you see on the screen. As much as you try to disguise how out of your depth you are by making the occasional confident 'uh huh', or 'yep, command D and shift, no problem', it's not long before he starts to realise. The pilot has been taken ill, and this poor sod is down in the control tower, trying to instruct a passenger over the radio how to land the plane. Oh, and all the engines have failed. And you're over the ocean. And you're deaf. That's how much you know about computers. Morgan always took care of this stuff for you, like he did for all the midwives at work. It was one of the reasons they loved him. Just one of them.

After a while the man exhausts his options.

'I'm afraid it seems it's encrypted,' he says.

'Right,' you say, 'now what?' He can hear your frustration. There is no way he can't. It buzzes through your knuckles, hums down the line.

'Well, because it's encrypted, you will need either . . . Morgan's permission,' deep breaths Colin, deep breaths, 'or a court order to proceed.'

'Why?'

'Well, because that's part of our terms and conditions.'

Your top lip lifts to expose your teeth.

'Stop being silly and help us,' you say.

The young man swallows, and for a second it's as though he's disappeared down his own throat.

'I'm so sorry,' he says, 'but you will need a court order.'

No way. You're done with courts. Done with solicitors. You're looking for an argument. It's been coming. You're too angry to even feel sorry for the poor bastard on the other end of the line, too sick of doing what you're told and sloping off, back into your dark little hole, licking your wounds, getting shafted, being disappointed with the outcome.

'Fuck that!' you say. You want answers, and this time you're going to get them.

You call the legal department of your union, who suggest you call the information commissioner in London, which you do, right that minute. You tell the man who answers the phone everything, a jet stream of frustration that almost melts his ear off.

'I can tell you now it's nothing to do with data protection,' he says. 'Your son died. His data is no longer protected. Apple are just being awkward and bloody-minded.'

'So it's not a legal requirement for them to do this?' you ask.

'Correct,' he says, and you smile a furious smile, because they don't show this, do they? They don't show this in their multi-million-dollar advertising campaigns, with the attractive young people dancing to music. It's hard to dance when you're being told that if you're out one night with your ear buds in and you're murdered in cold blood by a stranger, your family won't be able to access any of the art or music or memories you stored in the brand-new Apple device you queued up and paid good money for. How dare they treat you like this. How dare they keep a piece of Morgan from you. Well, you won't accept it. Not any more. You want everyone to hear.

So you decide to go to the press.

It's not just anger that makes you a pig-headed dick, you know. Sue will tell you. You're more than capable of being a pig-headed dick when you're calm too. But the anger definitely makes it worse. And that's why you ignore her suggestion to contact the *Mirror*. You want one of the serious papers to take your story and run with it. Not a tabloid. A broadsheet. One of those papers that unfolds like a blanket. So you get online and track down the number for the *Independent*. Then *The Times*. Then the *Guardian*. All the papers people have heard of. You try them all, but no one bites. So then you try the *Mirror*, who have a reporter call you back right away.

Sue gives you that look. You know the one. The 'I-was-right-and-you're-an-idiot' one. Yeah all right, bloody hell. But she doesn't gloat. She never does.

The reporter is interested in your story. He makes notes, asks questions. It's good tabloid fodder, after all. It's got a murder. A dead son. A stricken father. It's got . . .

He asks for a photograph of Morgan and a few family pictures. You feel sick with reluctance. Once the pictures are out there, they're out there, plastered across the internet for people to see and judge. But what are you going to do about it? You have to play the game. You *want* to play the game.

Finally, after all this time, you're going to make some noise. See if it drowns out the words that run through your head every night.

He slipped through the net.
Declan Gray slipped through the net.

Friday, 29 July 2016

The woman at the newsagent's glances at the five identical copies of today's *Mirror* in your hand with a slight look of pity. And to be fair, it does appear you've lost your mind. You've got this deranged expression on your face: part nerves, part excitement, part fear that it has all gone wrong.

But it hasn't.

When you stand outside the shop and open up the paper you see Morgan's face. The full beam of his smile. And the article is all about him, in a way the trial wasn't. In court it felt like they barely mentioned his name. But his name is all over this.

GRIEVING DAD SAYS APPLE WON'T GIVE HIM PASSWORD FOR MURDERED SON'S LAPTOP

You race home and find the article is live online too. And it feels good, seeing him there and knowing there are other people reading this, right now. It feels good that people are hearing your story. A heaviness lifts from you. Just a little, but enough.

You share the article on Facebook, but your list of 200 friends feels inadequate. So you click through to the handful of pages for music fans that you follow. It's just trivial stuff, people like you all over the world clinging to their youth by sharing songs they love. But that doesn't matter. It's still people. Thousands of them. So you share the link there too, with a little introduction you write quickly:

Could you imagine if Jim Morrison had composed music on his Apple Mac and died and Apple would not allow us to hear the music as it violates their terms and conditions? Could you re-post this story about what has happened to our son, he is a musician he has composed music on the MacBook and we want to access it.

The numbers go up. And up. And up.

Saturday, 30 July 2016

Maybe you're in the wrong profession. Maybe you should have been a radio DJ. All right, you're no Terry Wogan, but considering you're so nervous your voice keeps slipping into a high-pitched vibrato, you don't make too bad a job of your first radio interview. You answer all the questions the host on BBC Radio Coventry and Warwickshire throws at you, you don't swear in anger, and you tell everybody listening about how brilliant Morgan was. Which means you're doubly confident for the second interview of the day, with LBC, despite the prospect of a national audience, and a phone-in where listeners can share their views. And that too is going fine, until someone calls in to disagree with you. His point is that he wouldn't want his family to have access to his computer after his death. You're shocked, and for a few seconds you're on the ropes. It's not that you think everyone should have the same views as you. You're not that arrogant, despite this morning's taste of stardom. It's more that you can't believe there are people out there who'd call a radio phone-in show to have an argument with a grieving father whose son was murdered, and who just wants some bloody photographs and a bit of music back. Is anyone that big an arsehole?

The more you take your story out into the world, the more you'll meet them, these people who can't expand their horizons beyond their narrow world view. Well here's a little tip

163

from the future based on a quick inventory of everyone you'll ever meet from this day forth. Hopefully it'll save you a bit of time. These people . . . they're nearly always men, nearly always in their fifties, and they've got opinions on absolutely everything. And even though it's your son who died, they'll let you know it's them who're right about the way you should feel, the way you should act, the way you should grieve. And when you complain about them, Sue will jab you in the ribs with her elbow and point out you're not all that different, even though deep down she knows you are. Because it's true. To some people, your experience will never be more important than their desire to be heard.

Tuesday, 2 August 2016

They were there again, weren't they? Those words, in your head, the moment you woke up.

He slipped through the net.

Declan Gray slipped through the net.

For so long there was the sense you were drifting. Through the funeral. Through the trial. Through your grief. But now it's as though you're caught up in a giant snowball, getting faster, and bigger, and soon you'll be on national television telling everyone about Morgan at last and it feels right. Maybe this is what you need. Not just to hear the truth, but to speak it.

Sue hadn't wanted to come to the studio. When you first got the call she told you to do it on your own, and you agreed. Fair enough. No one should have to appear on television if they don't want to. But then she'd gone to work and told her friends and they'd all felt sorry for you, having to go it alone, so she'd had a change of heart and a compromise was struck.

She'd go with you on the train to Manchester, and stay in the hotel, and have a few beers in the bar before bed, and come to the studio first thing in the morning, but she wouldn't appear on TV. Not on your nelly.

It's still early when the make-up lady sweeps a soft brush across your forehead, which is a new experience, possibly for her too. How often do they stick slap on bereaved truck drivers? Admit it, though, it's not altogether unpleasant. There is an empty seat and a make-up lady with some unexpected free time so they do Sue too, which she enjoys, closing her eyes as though she's at a spa rather than in a tiny, brightly lit room, deep inside the belly of *BBC Breakfast* studios. Your stomach has started fluttering, like fish are fighting inside it. Six million people watch this show. Six million people are going to hear what you have to say, so you'd better make it bloody good.

In the green room there is coffee and orange juice and pastries, and there is a man reading a newspaper. He's wearing a suit and glasses, and is a little aloof at first, but after a while you get talking. Just small talk. A bit of this, a bit of that, and he's very articulate, which helps to distract you from what's ahead. He asks if this is your first time on TV, but surely he can tell by the way your feet won't stop tapping.

'Yes, very much so.'

Does he see your hand trembling?

'And why are you here?' he says.

You tell him about Morgan and the laptop. It's a good opportunity to rehearse before the cameras are rolling. The more clearly and concisely you explain it, the more people will understand your story, and ultimately that's the only thing that's important to you from this day forward. That everybody knows. The man mulls it over for a few seconds, as though he's working through a complex mathematical equation in his head.

'Hm,' he says, 'I wouldn't like my family to access my computer in the event of my death.' Sue squeezes your wrist with a pressure that translates as *whatever you do, don't say anything – not here, not now*, and miraculously, you manage to keep your mouth shut, smiling through pursed lips as you silently will the man to spill that steaming cup of coffee all over his balls seconds before he's due on air.

Thankfully, you're spared having to shake the man's hand when the show's host, Louise Minchin, comes out to greet you. She is lovely, her smile soothing.

'I'm so glad to meet you. Just relax,' she says, sensing your tension and expertly dispatching it. 'Is Sue going to talk to us too?'

As a matter of fact, Sue said she'd rather be eaten by a bloody lion than appear on national TV.

You're about to make an excuse but Sue steps forward, weaves her fingers through yours and nods.

'Yes, I'll say a few words.'

Do you remember your wedding vows? Kind of. They didn't reference this precise set of circumstances, as far as you recall, but you said something about being together through everything, no matter what. And you are. You need her now more than ever, and she's here, beside you. It can feel like you're apart, but you're not. You never will be, really.

Everyone says it when they go on television, don't they? But it's true. The set is smaller in real life, and the lighting so bright it takes a beat for your eyes to adjust. Charlie Stayt, the co-host, puts Sue at ease as you're ushered on to the red sofa you normally watch on TV. It's weird to think of the famous bums who've sat on it before you. And then, suddenly, you're on air. You're on the bloody air. Your face is being beamed out of televisions around the country. And people back home are plopping spoons down in milk-filled cereal bowls, saying:

'Did they just say Nuneaton?'

And, 'Aren't they the family who . . .'

And, 'Look, there's the couple that . . .'

And, 'Their son, isn't he the one who . . .'

And, 'I don't know how they coped with it, I really don't . . .'

But all you can think about is Sue. Isn't it funny? She only came to support you, and she wasn't even keen on doing that. Now, here she is, telling Morgan's story, about what happened to you, about his laptop, all on national TV. And she's doing so great that when they ask you a question you almost forget to answer, because where there were all the words you rehearsed, there's now a pride in your wife that six million people will see in your eyes, and they will know everything they need to know about your family when they do.

When it's over you call home. Connor and Eamon were watching, and they say it went well. And honestly? That's all you need to hear. Connor even takes a photo of the screen and posts it to his Instagram with the caption 'Fair play to them'.

Fair play to them! High praise indeed. Yeah. He's absolutely right about that. Fair play.

Wednesday, 7 September 2016

Detective Superintendent Adrian McGee ushers you and Sue into the meeting room at Nuneaton Police Station with a friendly smile and the quickly met promise of tea. He's new to the job and wasn't in it when Morgan was murdered, or through the subsequent investigation, he explains. You smile back, because he's a nice guy and you're a friendly person, still blissfully unaware of what's to come.

It was you who arranged a meeting with the police because there were niggling questions you needed answering. You hope they can blunt the needles of the words that jab in your flesh at night.

You know this: on 19 December 2011, Declan Gray, aged fifteen, was sentenced for manslaughter committed on 4 December 2010. He received a custodial sentence of fifty-four months in a young offenders' institution, to which the days he had already served on remand contributed. During this time Gray was released on licence but recalled to prison twice, once for breaching his licence conditions and once for a suspected involvement in an aggravated burglary, for which he was never charged. Gray was released from custody on 16 June 2015, having served the full term of his sentence.

It's what happened after that you don't know, and what you came here today to find out. How Declan Gray went on to murder your son.

He slipped through the net.

Declan Gray slipped through the net.

The police suggested you write your questions down and supply them in advance, so that they might be answered more definitively. Which is what you did. But what you hadn't realised is that this also means your hands are tied. If you think of another question now, you can't really ask it. Or you can, but the police will say they need time to prepare their response. You want the truth, but there's a crack forming between the question and the answer. The kind of crack that truth slips through.

Sue is one step ahead of you, though. When Detective Superintendent McGee starts to speak, she leans forward to say:

'Wait, can we have this all in writing?'

She's clever. She's suspicious. She's stubborn. Must be the Irish mother in her. You'd not thought that far ahead. Detective Superintendent McGee agrees.

Your first question was this:

'Who was responsible for the supervision of Declan Gray?'

Detective Superintendent McGee looks down at his paperwork.

'Gray was subject to Multi-Agency Public Protection Arrangements, or MAPPA, for the duration of his sentence. Due to his conviction for manslaughter, this was as a MAPPA "Category 2 Violent Offender". All Category 2 MAPPA offenders automatically exit MAPPA at their sentence expiry date. This does not necessarily mean that concerns are no longer present.'

It's hard to find a route through the jargon. You look deep into his eyes for a way.

'So there were concerns?'

Detective Superintendent McGee turns the page.

'In the case of Declan Gray . . . While there were appropriate concerns about the risks he would continue to pose upon release, there were no specific additional identifiable potential future victims that required safeguarding measures. Further, all agencies were already aware of the risks involved, so it was felt that proactive police management (outside of MAPPA) was appropriate. As the intelligence picture subsequently changed following Gray's release, further consideration for eligibility under MAPPA could have been considered. This does not appear to have happened.'

Wait, what?

You're mulling this over when Detective Superintendent McGee sips his tea and nods, as though to reassure you. And on some subconscious level, in this moment it works. Maybe it's his calm, maybe his authority, but you take a moment, blink, and move on to the next question.

'Was Gray cautioned, arrested, or known to the police after he was released in any capacity?'

Detective Superintendent McGee refers to his notes.

'On 14 December 2014, while out on licence from his manslaughter conviction, Declan Gray was arrested on suspicion of aggravated burglary, and released on bail. As he was on licence at the time, he was recalled to prison. Following further inquiries there was insufficient evidence to link Gray to the aggravated burglary and no further action was taken.'

That's the part you knew. It's the next part you'd no idea about. And you can tell it's important because Detective Superintendent McGee pauses before he answers, as though he's taking a run-up.

'Since he completed his sentence and had not been subject to any supervision order, Declan Gray was arrested and released without charge on the following three occasions: on 16 June 2015, on suspicion of wounding. On 13 September 2015, on suspicion of theft in a dwelling and a wounding. On 9 October 2015, on suspicion of fear of provocation or violence. On each occasion, there was insufficient evidence and/or a lack of co-operation from witnesses/victims to prosecute . . .'

Wait . . . he was arrested three times between being released and murdering Morgan?

The blood drains from your face. You feel it rush downwards through your body. Sue leans forward, interrupts him. Bloody hell, she's good at this.

'So he was out on the streets until he did something *really* bad?'

Detective Superintendent McGee looks embarrassed, and you can see it in his eyes: he sort of agrees with her. A tacit agreement over the awful truth about what this means. If Declan Gray, who while in prison for manslaughter had been categorised as a violent offender, had been supervised on his release, just as the changing 'intelligence picture' suggested should have happened . . . maybe he wouldn't have been free to murder Morgan. But because Declan Gray finished his sentence he wasn't supervised at all – as though, by magic, he was exorcised of violence the moment he walked out of the prison gates.

Whereas, in fact, the very opposite was true. Declan Gray was full of violence, just as he had been when he entered the prison system. And, free for the first time as an adult, he wasn't being watched by those invested with the power to protect the people. Equally, if – on any of the three occasions when he was arrested, while unmonitored, in the four and a half months between finishing his sentence for manslaughter and murdering Morgan – the police had found sufficient evidence or a co-operating witness that allowed them to prosecute him, Declan Gray might, and maybe should, have been in prison on the night he murdered Morgan.

Either Sue takes your hand or you take hers, you're not sure, you just kind of meld, made amorphous by grief, as you have been so often lately. But you emerge unsettled by a new sensation you can't shake. The feeling that there's something you're not being told. That the truth still evades you, or, behind the smiles and tea, is being obscured.

THE GOOGLE SEARCH HISTORY OF A
BEREAVED FATHER

Murder
Knife crime
Government stats murder

Young people knife crime
Government stats murder young people
Crime Nuneaton
Morgan Hehir

Saturday, 17 September 2016

You drive and drive and drive, through the cross-stitch of countryside that cleaves into valleys, and it feels not like a journey but a pilgrimage. Like you're looking for answers, but you don't yet know the right questions to ask.

'How long has it been since your son died?' Clive asks. He runs the British Ironwork Centre in Oswestry, near the Welsh border. All this – the sculptures, the café, the arts and crafts shops – it's his, and he's charming and charismatic and searching your eyes for the real reason you've come, though you're not even sure what it is.

'About ten months,' you say. He nods.

'It's very soon.'

It strikes you as a weird thing to say, but only because you don't yet realise. He's seen eyes like yours before. The absence of light in them. How far behind them you are.

You, Sue and Eamon finish your coffees and follow Clive through a doorway into a huge room, where the *Knife Angel* stands above you. For a moment, like your pain, it is too big to hold inside.

At twenty-seven feet tall, and constructed from over 100,000 knives collected in a nationwide amnesty, the National Monument Against Violence and Aggression is a gigantic sculpture of an angel. It has giant wings, each a cascade of fanned blades that catch the sun and shimmer like feathers. Its hands are turned upwards to God.

Clive gives you a meat cleaver and asks if you'd like to inscribe a message on it. It feels awful and odd and reminds you of those old westerns, of bullets with names on. But you do it because you need to do something for Morgan.

Eamon films you on the GoPro. One day soon you'll send the footage to the local newspaper, and when you do, a local reporter, Claire Harrison, who covered Morgan's murder and will remain a friend of your family, will ask the Nuneaton police force how many knives were put into their own amnesty bin and have since been added to the *Knife Angel*.

They will discover that there are no blades from Nuneaton at all. Maybe that's the answer you sought.

Friday, 30 September 2016

You're at work when your phone vibrates in your pocket. It's difficult to remember the last time that little burst against your thigh meant good news. You're greeted by a photograph Sue has sent – not of herself but of a stranger, sitting on your sofa. On his face is a huge smile, and in his hands a MacBook.

After your appearance on *BBC Breakfast*, and in the absence of any assistance from Apple, a few people had been in touch to say they might be able to help you access Morgan's laptop, and all of his art, music, film and photographs from the cloud. But you couldn't bear the thought of handing it over to someone you didn't know. Which is why Sue said yes when she got a message from Steve, an old friend and colleague of Morgan's, who said he not only knew someone who might be able to do it, but that they could come to the house that evening.

Steve arrived a few hours later with his friend Mike, a paramedic who had just finished his shift and was still in uniform, which is maybe why Sue felt she could trust him straight away. Mike said he was really into computers and seemed to relish the challenge, but Sue remained unconvinced. She'd tried everything over the past month, and without Apple's compliance, it had started to feel like she was sitting outside Fort Knox.

But Steve and Mike, bless them, were unperturbed. They sat in your lounge, enthusiastically thinking their way around every failed attempt, trying every possible thing that could be tried, until three hours later there was a breakthrough, thanks largely to a moment of inspiration on Sue's part, and Morgan's art, music, film and photographs suddenly appeared. Sue was euphoric. It meant the world to her, that these two young men cared enough to not give up. That they'd helped her see her son again.

The timing was especially poignant. You'd just received a letter back from your MP, Marcus Jones, giving you more bad news, only now on Houses of Parliament paper, which somehow made it even more difficult to swallow. He said he'd made inquiries in London, and that because Apple is a private company nominally based in Ireland (let's face it, for tax reasons, not the craic), there was nothing he could do to compel them to give you access to Morgan's data, though he was intending to contact the Irish government to see if Apple did the same for its citizens.

You haven't the heart to tell him you're looking at a photograph Sue took of Mike's victory while dancing around the lounge. Partly because, who knows, maybe he can help people, and partly because you still grapple with a little of that old Catholic guilt now and again. But it ebbs away as you watch Sue spend the evening looking through Morgan's photographs, watching silly videos he made for the amusement of his friends, and listening to music he recorded and which you didn't even know existed until now.

How sweet, to hear his fingers slide down the strings of a bass guitar. To see her smile when they do.

Wednesday, 12 October 2016

The arrival of autumn makes you long for time to travel backwards. For the leaves to turn from brown to green and leap back on to the trees. To come back to life. It'll be the anniversary of Morgan's death soon, and the shift in seasons is shrouded in warning. You're going to need help to stay strong.

Olivia was the one who told you about The Moira Fund. It was set up by a woman named Bea Jones in memory of her daughter, Moira, who was raped and murdered in a Glasgow park in May 2008. Bea ran the charity to help other families traumatically bereaved by the murder of a loved one. To buy them some respite, a chance to escape, albeit briefly, from their grief. It had been the fund that paid for you and Sue to take Eamon and his girlfriend on a trip to the Olympic Park Slide, which you went down so fast you feared you might get the bends. Eamon laughed about that for longer than it took you to travel the 178 metres top to bottom.

You call Bea to thank her.

'Does it get any easier?' you ask.

You hear her fall silent on the other end of the line, and you imagine her flicking through a Rolodex of grief. The children she's helped cope when a father has killed a mother. The flowers she helped them buy for the funeral. The new coat and shoes.

'No,' she says, 'it doesn't.'

And you know she's right, don't you? You don't have to get over it. You can't. You just have to keep going.

Keep going.

Tuesday, 25 October 2016

It's just plastic. That's all. Just junk. You load it into the truck from the warehouse, and you load it into the store from the truck, and you remind yourself again. It's just plastic. Just nonsense. Just tat. But it makes panic swarm inside you to see pumpkins and witches' hats and Frankenstein masks, and the whole business of Halloween on every shelf in every shop you enter, and soon, on every door you pass, a fake cobweb and a sign that says beware.

But it comes for you anyway, the panic. You grip the wheel and lock the doors of your truck, all 100,000 of the *Knife Angel*'s blades above you, your name writ large on each.

Saturday, 29 October 2016

It's the weekend.

The weekend.

There is you, Sue, Connor, Eamon, Craig, Dave, Stevie, Joe and Millie, all the people Morgan loved most, in a lodge at Center Parcs, surrounded by trees. There's a pool table, where all these men half your age say they're going to beat you and mostly do. There's a pool to swim in and a badminton net and all these ways to distract yourself from what this weekend really is – the anniversary of Morgan's death.

There's a huge lounge, where you can all be together. Where you can talk about Morgan or not talk about Morgan. You can cry or not cry. Everybody is comfortable here. Everybody can make up their own mind about how they get through this, the end of the first year without him.

And you? You talk and listen and laugh and cry. And you drink. And you drink. And you drink. And when you drink, you black out.

It's been happening a lot recently, and it's happening again now. You're fine after one. Two is OK. But after three or four, your mind runs down into your body. Your muscles grow heavy. Your bones become wood. You're ravaged by a fatigue that bends you into something new and useless. Connor is talking to you, and you're trying to be attentive, but the chair on which you sit is meshing with your flesh. You are becoming inanimate. He's saying something, and it's not that you're not listening. It's that you can't. It's that you're no longer there.

Monday, 31 October 2016

Anything to not be on the sofa, looking at the clock as it ticks past 9.30, now, a year ago, forever.

A TRAGEDY IN NUNEATON: PART THREE
THE 23.30 RAIL DISASTER

The 23.30 sleeper train from London Euston to Glasgow was approaching Nuneaton over an hour late. Work was being done to remodel the track around the station, which in the sticky summer of 1975 was always busy with traffic on the

West Coast Main Line. Nuneaton now had a population of over 70,000, an increasing number of whom commuted to nearby Coventry and Birmingham for work. The town had simply outgrown its infrastructure, and its rail network needed regeneration fast.

The train driver should have seen an advance-warning board placed at the standard service braking distance of a mile and a quarter before the temporary speed-restricted zone of 20 mph. But he didn't. Though it was the dead of night – 1.54 a.m., to be precise – and the advance-warning board should have been illuminated, it was not.

The driver would state at a later inquest that, because the advance-warning board was cast in darkness, he assumed the speed restriction had been lifted, and as such didn't need to slow down. Which was why he drove the train through the next mile and a quarter at 80 mph. It was not until he saw the correctly illuminated commencement board whip by that he realised the speed restriction was still in place. By then he was moving 60 mph too fast, and although he applied the emergency brakes, it was already too late.

The train sped into a sharply curved length of temporary track, tearing the two Class-86 electric locomotives apart. The first stayed on the track, eventually coming to a stop halfway through Nuneaton station. The second veered sideways, striking, then mounting, the northbound platform, where it collided with the platform canopy and was brought to a sudden and violent halt. The twelve coaches behind it, carrying just under 100 sleeping passengers, immediately derailed, zig-zagging across the tracks. While the first two remained upright, carriages three, four and five were flipped on to their sides and crushed.

Six people – four passengers and two staff – died that night. Thirty-eight were injured, and lucky to be alive.

If there was a glimmer of good fortune in a catastrophe that sent the town into shock when it woke later that morning, it was that the train had been far from full.

The inquest found that the advance-warning board was not illuminated because the equipment that powered it had been set up incorrectly. When one gas cylinder ran empty, a valve was meant to automatically switch the supply to a second. But the valve had not been used. The first ran out of gas shortly after 1.10 a.m. that morning, sealing the fates of the passengers fast approaching in the darkness.

A number of recommendations to prevent a recurrence of the accident were accepted by the British Railways Board, the primary one being the installation of temporary Automatic Warning System magnets at locations affected by speed restrictions so drivers were given audible notice. It would ensure that a tragedy like this could never happen again. That there wouldn't be another night as dark.

Friday, 17 February 2017

Detective Superintendent Adrian McGee sits on the sofa, opening a thick file of documents and carefully leafing through. You've become used to people in your lounge, drinking your tea, stoking your agony. But these visits are dwindling. They are fewer, further apart, and one day there will be none. You can't escape the feeling that Nuneaton is getting over this tragedy, because it has to. And you don't like it. Uh-uh. You don't want Morgan's memory to become just another plaque on the wall. Not like the one unveiled at the train station, two months before he died. The one that marked forty years since another tragedy the town had no choice but to move beyond.

But you'll do well to think of that disaster and its inquest when Detective Superintendent McGee finally gets to the purpose of his visit. Think of the way the real truth – when it emerged, when it was forced out – changed the system and saved others, as he starts to go through your list of questions again, the ones about Declan Gray leaving prison unsupervised, the ones you already asked him at the police station.

When it dawns on you what's happening, you and Sue do some long-married-couple telepathy, both of you asking, simultaneously and silently, is this for fucking real? Why is he just repeating what you've already heard? Is this to make you stop asking? Are they trying to bore you out of the picture? To dazzle you with process? To make you accept what's already been said? Is this to make you go away?

You've repeatedly emailed to remind them about getting written answers and been fobbed off every time. It feels like you're hitting a wall. Like you're banging your head against it.

'I thought you were going to put these in writing?' Sue says, with those heart-stopping serious eyes she gets when she's not taking any more shit. You really wouldn't want to be Detective Superintendent McGee right now.

'I will,' he says, 'I just had a few problems.' The way it slides from his mouth, as though escaping, feels like an excuse. Sue's voice in your head agrees. Fuck this.

You show Detective Superintendent McGee out to his car with a smile and a friendly but businesslike handshake. No, you won't stop asking. No, you won't go away. As soon as you get the answers in writing, you'll get on the phone to the media, and make a noise the whole town will hear. If the police won't tell you what you want to know – exactly how and why Declan Gray was free the night he killed Morgan – then you'll force it out of them, because there is something inside you screaming that they made a mistake, and that no one is telling you what it is.

Thursday, 6 April 2017

Your face is red. Bright red. Close to molten. You can see your cheeks glowing like a couple of bloody distress beacons any time you look at anything below your nose. It's not like it's the first time. This happens when you're nervous, and it's natural. Almost all living creatures have a tell. Even Siamese fighting fish have been found to let out a kind of yawn just before a scrap that scientists believe is a sign of nerves. And they're fish, for Christ's sake. So it's perfectly acceptable to be able to see you're nervous from space, considering you're standing on a stage, next to the Mayor of Nuneaton, in the grand main chamber of the Council House, where a packed crowd are waiting for you to say a few words.

'Welcome,' you say, 'to the first annual Morgan awards.'

You had the idea early on, both as a way of keeping Morgan's name alive and as a thank you to the good people of the town, who'd been so kind to you, coming together as a community to help you financially through the aftermath of Morgan's death. Claire, the reporter at the *Nuneaton News*, had printed forms in the paper, so that readers could fill them in and send them off to nominate worthy winners. Craig and Joe designed a logo, and you even got eight-inch-tall glass trophies made for the winners, which you're pleased to report look pretty classy, and not just like the kind of thing someone might use to prop open the downstairs toilet door.

You hand out the awards to the winners, with a special one for Jack, nominated by you and Sue for the effort he made raising all that money.

At the end, the mayor comes and whispers in your ear.

'I think you did a really good job.'

'Thanks,' you say. 'Just as well I didn't go red.'

She awkwardly looks down at the bright-pink hue of your skin reflected in her ton of ceremonial necklace.

'It's OK,' you say. 'I know my face is really red. It's burning.'

She laughs a laugh so big it's kind of mayoral too, and when you're finally alone you think to yourself: we should do this every year.

Tuesday, 2 May 2017

You can try to ignore the BBC *Midlands Today* camera crew poking out from behind that tree all you like, but deep down you're relatively sure you're doing that 'Oh-Jesus-Christ-I'm-on-television' walk people do when they know they're being filmed, as though everything they learned about walking was from hearsay. When you finally received Detective Superintendent McGee's written answers by email, the first thing you did was contact Claire at the *Nuneaton News*, and then Louisa Currie, the BBC's local reporter. It was her idea – a great one, you thought – to do the interview here in Pool Bank Street Rec, retracing Morgan's last steps.

LOUISA CURRIE: Colin's son Morgan was killed here, at Pool Bank Street Recreation Ground in Nuneaton.

COLIN HEHIR: He just wanted to enjoy and experience life. Make everybody smile, make everybody laugh. That was just his way. He was a caring person.

The two of you walk along the pathway through the park, filmed from a distance. Far enough away for people watching on TV not to see the effort you're putting into looking relaxed.

LOUISA CURRIE: Three men have been jailed in connection with Morgan's death. Declan Gray is serving life for murder. He had been released from prison four months earlier, but having served his full sentence for a previous killing, he was released without supervision. He was arrested for violence three times before Morgan's death but never charged. Colin fears there's nothing to stop the same thing happening again.

You're sitting on a bench now. The camera is not all that far from your face, but it doesn't matter. You barely notice it. You've hit your stride. You're saying what you want everybody to hear.

COLIN HEHIR: I'd like some kind of a review or investigation into . . . was everything done that could have been done to prevent Morgan's death?

The camera guys peel away, taking bleak footage of the Rec to intersperse with the interview under Louisa's narration.

LOUISA CURRIE: The park is somewhere he visits when he feels angry.

COLIN HEHIR: I just feel so emotional. It's the place where Morgan took his last steps on that night. It does fill me with anxiety and dread to walk through here. But I feel the need to come here. I can't stay away.

Once the interview is over, Louisa and the cameraman agree you did well. Maybe they're just being polite, but you'll take it. You need all the confidence you can get ahead of Thursday. She has somehow convinced Detective Superintendent McGee to allow himself to be interviewed by you, on camera. You don't say this, because you're a gentleman and she works for the BBC, but you're shitting yourself. Maybe she can tell by the way you swallow your nerves like a fishbone.

'I think you'll be good at it,' she says.

'No pressure there then,' you say, and they all laugh.

Thursday, 4 May 2017

'Don't look at the camera,' the cameraman says, and immediately you look at the camera. You've got that warm-leg feeling you sometimes get when you're nervous, as though your body is somewhere between slumber and flames. There are a few minutes to wait while they set up their shot, so you look out across the golf course that rolls around The Warwickshire health club, hotel and spa, next to the Police Headquarters in Leek Wootton. Hard to deny it's anything other than bad optics for those inclined to suspect the police force is headed by powerful white men making secret handshakes as they amble down the back nine.

You straighten your tie, smooth down your suit jacket, tuck your folder beneath your arm and walk through the grand doors of the HQ while they film you. It feels entirely staged, which it is, and the more they make you do it, the less natural it becomes. On the fourth attempt, the cameraman declares he's got the shot. Strange, because you're sure you walked like John Wayne the morning after his first visit to a personal trainer.

The meeting room is big and eerily bare. You sit down opposite two empty chairs, your stomach twisting into ribbons as you slide your list of questions from the folder.

'It's OK to read from a piece of paper,' the cameraman says, 'but don't keep looking down, it won't look good.'

Detective Superintendent McGee enters with Warwickshire Police and Crime Commissioner, Philip Seccombe. The top man. They sit down, and maybe you don't see it, maybe you're staring at the piece of paper already, but they're uncomfortable too. Your pain is difficult to peer into. Or maybe it's just the cameras. You swap a few pleasantries, and then, encouraged by the crew, get straight to the point.

'I believe Morgan's death was preventable with some form of police intervention,' you say.

'Yes,' Mr Seccombe says. He's got a statesmanlike manner. 'You were let down by the system. I'm not blaming the police, but you have had a bad outcome, and a bad result.'

'Sometimes,' says Mr McGee, 'we will get it wrong. And I've said before, the apology is always there. I don't know if we could have done anything different that would have got to a different result . . .'

Are you being too controlled? Too wooden? Too stilted? Should you leap from your seat and throw it through the window? It's all happening so fast, you can't tell. You interrupt.

'That's what I . . . I think that's the only lesson I'm gonna learn if we get to the bottom of that, whether there were mistakes. And identify where these were.'

All you know for sure is you half garbled that, you hate every minute of this, and you feel deeply unsatisfied.

'We should look into this,' Mr Seccombe says, 'we should learn the lessons. And we should try and stop this happening again.'

The interview lasts a paltry ten minutes, and at the end, as you're made to shake hands three times for the cameras, you can't help but feel you've blown it. The Police and Crime Commissioner says his office will be in touch soon – which is what you want, you want them to look into it – and the joy and relief this brings drowns out the voice in your head telling you that you missed your chance.

But you didn't. You watch it go out on TV, expecting a trove of ammunition Sue can use to take the piss. But it's good. It's very good. They've cut out all the ums and ahs. All the duff questions. All the stilted moments. Nobody is about to offer you your own primetime TV interview show, but the Police and Crime Commissioner said you've been let down by the system, even if the police won't take the blame. And that must merit a review, an inquiry, surely?

He'll be in touch. That's what he said. Suddenly, you feel the wind behind you. Suddenly, the drums you play are loud.

COVENTRY TELEGRAPH
FATHER OF MURDERED MORGAN CALLS FOR REVIEW AFTER REVEALING KILLER HAD BEEN ARRESTED 3 TIMES IN 4 MONTHS BEFORE FATAL STABBING

By CLAIRE HARRISON Nuneaton Reporter

A NUNEATON dad whose son was tragically murdered has claimed his family were let down by the system. Morgan Hehir's murderer was a convicted killer who was released from prison and arrested THREE times in the four months before he took Morgan's life.

Colin Hehir says the cruel killer was a 'ticking time bomb' and is now calling for a review into how the police prevent criminals reoffending.

His comments come almost a year after his son's killer was handed a life-sentence for murdering hospital worker Morgan just four months after he was released from prison. Colin wants to close a loophole that he believes led to the murder of his ever-smiling, fun-loving son Morgan.

Having kept tight-lipped for the past 12 months, Colin has ended his silence about how convicted killer Declan Gray was allowed to murder his beloved son despite being arrested for another violent incident involving a knife just weeks before.

Gray was arrested three times in the four months between him being released from prison and cruelly taking the life of the 20-year-old in Pool Bank Street on Halloween night back in 2015. On each occasion the victim did not want to press charges, so no police action could be taken.

Having completed his full sentence for a previous conviction for manslaughter, under Government guidelines Declan was not being supervised.

'He (Declan) was like a ticking time bomb, it was only a matter of time before he seriously hurt someone, but it seemed that they (the police) could not do anything until he actually killed someone,' Colin said. Now Colin wants a review or an independent inquiry to be held into his son's case, and to close the loophole that allows some convicted killers to be released from prison without supervision.

'Ultimately it is too late for us, the damage has been done, it is irreparable but we never want this to happen to another family,' he said.

'The police are saying that they couldn't do any more, but I would just like a review into it.

'The whole system is geared towards supporting the criminal, it forgets the victim, they (the criminals) are so well kept in terms of their rights, but what about the victim's rights? If someone is dangerous, and has shown patterns of violence, surely something could have been or should be done to keep an eye on them.

'Just look at Declan's previous convictions, he was done for manslaughter, the system presumes that he is going to be rehabilitated but where is the plan B, if he isn't rehabilitated – he is just let out on to the streets again to wait for him to do something again.'

He put his concerns to Warwickshire's Police and Crime Commissioner Philip Seccombe and Detective Superintendent Adrian McGee, head of the Major Investigations Unit at Warwickshire Police Force, who led the investigation into Morgan's murder.

'It was difficult for me to do, but this is what I have been wanting to do for 12 months, to try and get the answers we did not get in court,' he said. 'All we got in court was role play, they (Declan Gray, Karlton Gray and Simon Rowbotham) just threw their cards in and took the sentence, none of them took to the stand. The police sympathised with me and said that we had been let down by the system, but I want them to look into the system and see if anything can be done to stop this from happening again.'

The Commissioner was contacted and Mr Seccombe agreed that he would organise a meeting with all of the agencies to look into the situation.

'I met last week with Mr Hehir to discuss his concerns around the circumstances which led up to Morgan's death and I have agreed to look into them further on his behalf. There are well-documented procedures for monitoring offenders on release from prison and, while it appears all agencies followed these in the case of Declan Gray, there are questions as to whether the processes for monitoring violent offenders after they have served their full term of imprisonment are currently adequate.

That last part sticks in your craw. Like they've looked into it already. Like you're meant to be satisfied with that. Like there is nothing else to know.

But that's not how you feel.

Friday, 5 May 2017

The numbers go up and up and up. You posted the BBC *Midlands Today* clip on YouTube, and now every time you check there are more likes and more shares. You stay up late – way too late, must be one in the morning – watching the comments unfurl beneath your Facebook post about the interview on the Nuneaton Community forum. It feels good to have everything laid out before its 20,000 members. Feels good to watch the numbers rise. As though you're reanimating their interest. Not letting the town's memory fade.

You look at the moonlight dappling the lawn and finally concede it's time for bed. But then you get a private message from a woman you don't know. She has watched the BBC clip, and read the *Coventry Telegraph* article, and she says your information is not true.

Now you know, don't you, that there are people out there who prey on families touched by tragedy like yours. People who take a perverse delight in crowbarring themselves in, exploiting the desperation of those who've lost everything just for kicks. You've seen documentaries about them. People who phone police hotlines to say they have vital information. Who mould their joy from the wet clay of false hope. And you're wary, of course you are, because it'll be a cold day in hell before your family are dragged through any more unnecessary pain; that's the vow you've made to yourself.

But this. This seems different. You've a couple of shared Facebook friends. The woman lives in Nuneaton. She's not anonymous. There's every chance you could go to the market in town on a Saturday and stand next to her buying bread. So you float the cursor over her message. You hold your breath. And the hairs rise on your neck.

She says she has a relative who was attacked by Declan Gray after he was released from prison, before he murdered Morgan.

You knew Gray was arrested three times in that window. This must be one of those. The last of his arrests. This isn't new, not really. But hold on, that's not what she said. She said the information wasn't true.

You message back at 1.12 a.m. Look at how polite you are. How understanding. Despite everything this might mean, the way your hands tremble so hard as you type that the keys rattle, you're still you.

Hi. I don't want to pry too much but would you be able to tell me what happened to your relative? If you don't want to tell me I understand and it's not a problem. Thank you.

You press send, sit back and wait. But there's no response. Not even that blinking ellipsis that means someone is there, thinking, writing. Maybe you've scared her off. Maybe it's time to go to bed.

But in the morning, there's a reply.

He was out riding his skateboard and was approached by Declan. There was a disagreement involving Declan (sorry to have to use his name) pulling out a knife and chasing him and the victim managed to escape and call the police. They arrived quickly and managed to arrest him before a PC took a statement and later that night came back to say that there was insufficient evidence. They did not call to say that Declan had been released without charge, and they crossed paths the next day. There was a complaint made via the non-police emergency number and they said that without a crime reference number they couldn't do anything.

You freeze in the centre of the lounge. The blood rushes from your head, into your feet, weighs your body down as you leap up out of it, as though you are your own scream.

'On each occasion the victim did not want to press charges, so no police action could be taken.' That's what you were told. But this woman, her family, they'd wanted to press charges. They'd called to speak to someone. And they weren't even given a crime reference number. They were told they couldn't do anything.

What you were told was not the truth.

I am so sorry this has happened. It still shocks me to this day. I worked with Morgan for a little while and he was a lovely lad. For what it's worth I wish with all my heart that the police had done more.

Wednesday, 28 June 2017

You sit in the reception of Leek Wootton Police HQ and imagine yourself as a fireball. You'd been hoping that when the Police and Crime Commissioner's office got in touch it would be about a review of the case. You had not expected him to invite you to the MAPPA meeting he'd convened with all the agencies responsible for monitoring people released from prison. You're not even totally sure what it's about. But you're here now, being ushered into the room where you interviewed him on camera, the smells of well-brewed tea and furniture polish hanging in the air. You're here now and you won't be extinguished. You want to leave with the promise of an inquiry into the police's interactions with Declan Gray before he murdered Morgan.

There are twelve, maybe fourteen people around a rectangular table that has a hole in the middle, like a tiny Colosseum. Mr Seccombe asks everyone to take it in turns to introduce themselves, and they do, their names, and the agency they represent. The Youth Offending Services, the Police, the Crown Prosecution Service, the Probation Service, the Prison Service, the Police and Crime Commissioner himself and two solicitors from Warwickshire County Council. MAPPA.

'OK,' Mr Seccombe says, 'Colin, it's over to you.'

You had no idea that was about to happen. You've no speech prepared. Not even any notes. All you can think is that you've had dreams like this – nightmares, really. Where you're meant to do something important but have no clue what. Where you wake iced in cold sweat.

But now? Right now, you don't fear anything.

You reach into your bag and take out a framed photograph of Morgan, standing it up proudly on the table so everyone can see him. Your boy.

'Has anyone had a chance to watch my video?' you ask. They all start nodding.

The video. You spent the past few weeks since you were invited to this meeting teaching yourself how to use Vimeo. You uploaded the footage you took walking Morgan's last steps with a camera pointed at your own face and sent the link to the Police and Crime Commissioner for him to forward to each agency, with plenty of time for them to watch. Sue thought you were crazy, and maybe you were. But they're still nodding at the MAPPA meeting, even though you checked this morning before leaving the house and know for a fact nobody has watched the video. It says as much beneath it. A number that hasn't changed.

'Right, there's no point in me talking about that then,' you say. There's a heat in your words but a coldness in your eyes. 'So instead, let me tell you about Morgan's last day alive.'

You don't need notes for this. It's seared right through you. For ten unbroken minutes, without a stammer or a stumble, you talk them through the events of Saturday, 31 October 2015, from eating bacon and eggs in the morning to the moment two tired strangers sat down opposite you in a hospital room and said there was nothing they could do to save your son's life. And you let that hang in the air while you look each and every one of them in the eye. This is how the decisions they make might get someone killed. The room stays quiet until you sit back down.

It's someone else's turn to speak then, about what their agency has been doing recently. That's when it dawns on you. None of these people are here to listen to what happened to Morgan, or to figure out what, if anything, went wrong. They're here because they've been invited by the Police and Crime Commissioner to see if there are systemic problems that can be fixed before someone else like Declan is released into the community. They're here to talk about the future, not the past. About other sons, sons still alive. Not yours. And you? Your invitation was a kind of peace offering, a placatory gesture that is in fact anything but.

'All right,' you say, uninvited. 'Tell me what will be different when Karlton Gray is released?'

Wait a second. Did you hear that? Did you imagine it? You could *swear* one of the men from the Prison Service said 'nothing' under his breath. The head of the Probation Service for Coventry, Solihull and Warwickshire, Andy Wade, takes the baton, explaining they would like to have worked with Declan for longer, but they were unable to because he served his full sentence. He looks down at his file and reads:

'Declan had started turning things around. He was off drugs and had a new girlfriend and was going to the gym.'

But that report he's reading is from when Declan Gray was released early from his prison sentence for his man-slaughter conviction, before he was recalled on licence for bad behaviour. When he was being monitored. Not from when he was released after finishing his sentence, when he killed Morgan, when he wasn't monitored at all. It's not a lie, but it's information given out of context. And it works, doesn't it, because for a second you sit back in your seat, a little confused, a little overwhelmed. You feel like a pest.

But a pest is what you want to be. So you stand up again, reach into your bag and you take out ten printed copies of the Facebook message you received which states that when Declan was arrested for allegedly threatening someone with a knife, just weeks before Morgan was killed, the victim had wanted to press charges, contrary to everything you've been told. You walk round the table, firmly placing a copy down in front of each representative.

'Here,' you say. 'If this message is true, Declan Gray would never have been able to murder Morgan.'

You know it's not proof. You know it's not evidence. But it's something, isn't it? It's something they need to look into. It's something that merits an inquiry, a report, anything.

The room falls silent. So quiet you can hear long blinks, slow swallows, the parting of dry lips. You sink back into your seat, where no one dares look at you for fear they'll see what by now they must sense. You, breaking.

'Mr Hehir,' Mr Seccombe says. It might be two minutes later, might be two hours, you're not sure. 'Would you like to say a few words to close the meeting?'

Go on. Scream it.

Do something!

But you open your mouth, and it comes out so meekly you wonder if it came out at all.

'We have to try and improve things so what's happened to us doesn't happen again.' That's what you say. That's what you say before you leave with nothing.

Here's what will happen. On glorious summer mornings, when you're out on your bike across the fields and it seems the sun has risen just for you, you'll allow it to fill you with hope. Hope that one of the people from the agencies will have picked up your sheet of paper with the Facebook message printed out, taken it away and read it and thought about it and realise you might have been lied to. Hope that they might do something after all. You'll take that hope and keep it burning like a pilot light you shield from the wind. When it flickers, you'll email the Police and Crime Commissioner's office asking if they've done anything about the message. But over and over again, as the weeks and months pass, they'll fob you off with some excuse or other – we're training new staff, we'll get back to you soon – and every time they do, the hope gutters. Out of desperation, you'll ask Claire at the newspaper to try on your behalf. She'll contact the Police and Crime Commissioner's office too, and she'll hit the same wall. They will send her a press release about some new Community Order training they've arranged. It'll be so dull she won't even write it up.

But you don't stop asking. You don't stop sending emails. You don't stop calling. Hope is not the same as need.

In Morgan's school leavers' book, every pupil wrote a message. These days it always flops open on his page. But even someone with no idea who Morgan was, who didn't yearn to see him every day, would find themselves drawn to his face among the others: his skin that much pinker, his cheeks that much rounder, his smile that much wider.

Most pupils have responded to the question 'What is your ambition?' in the same way: to travel the world, to find success in their chosen career, or to have a big and happy family.

But not Morgan. Beneath Morgan's name, it simply says, 'I want to have a pet dog called Jimmy.'

You read it and you read it again, and at first you think: that's typical Morgan that is. Messing around. Making people laugh. Not taking anything seriously. But then you remember a conversation you had one night. You were sitting watching TV, you and Sue and each of your three sons in their favourite chairs. They were safe, so you were happy. Out of the corner of your eye you noticed Morgan looking up at Connor, a man already, and down at Eamon, fast becoming one. At you and Sue, with the lines round your eyes got from loving them. And he was smiling to himself, as though seeing, as young men must for the first time at that age, the passing of the years and how it sculpts the dunes, while remaining, in their minds, immune to the very same winds.

'Dad,' he said.

'Uh huh,' you said, pretending your eyes had been on the screen the whole time.

'I bet you get a dog when we all leave home.'

And you remember those words again as you walk through the front door with Jimmy, tiny Jimmy, in your arms.

One night, not long back, you'd caught a documentary about soldiers returning from war with PTSD, and the difference dogs made to their lives. You want that. You want something that will change the mood in the house. Something that will be genuinely happy to see you when you come home. Something with no knowledge of your pain and no pain of its own.

Jimmy runs the ticklish wafer of his springer spaniel tongue across your cheek and dashes in a crazed loop around the kitchen. Sue has told you in no uncertain terms that she won't be looking after him, and in no circumstances whatsoever will she be picking up his poo. He's your dog, and that's that. But now he's here, she's smiling to herself, and then she's stroking him, tugging on his ear just the way he likes, and soon she's holding him in her arms, even though, in her words, he's a knob who keeps eating her shoes.

You'd like to be able to say Jimmy has something of Morgan's spirit in him, but you don't feel that way. And that's all right. It's OK to want something to need you. It's OK to need something to keep your hope aflame.

Monday, 12 February 2018

The Office of the Police and Crime Commissioner in Warwick is housed in a beautiful Regency building where large windows blanket warm rooms in slabs of winter light. Not the kind of place you'd pictured having a confrontation, but you'll take it. You were so sick of waiting that now you've come to them. And this time you're not going to politely request an inquiry, you're going to demand one.

The Police and Crime Commissioner himself is on holiday at the moment, the kind receptionist says, and you can't blame him for that what with this weather you suppose, even if it is a bit galling to be met with an ever-changing cast. But the young woman assures you that his deputy, Neil Tipton, who you remember from the MAPPA meeting, will be with you soon, as will his colleague Zeynab.

Hang on.

Is that—

No, you're just being paranoid. But through a door at the end of a corridor you think you see Michael and Lara. The two solicitors from Warwickshire County Council who attended the MAPPA meeting. And they're talking to Neil and Zeynab. Are they having a meeting about how to deal with you? That's the first thing you think, and it makes you focus. You need to be on top of your game. You open your folder and reread as many documents as you can to refresh your memory. In situations like this, when your adrenalin is up, it can feel like you need rebooting. You're worse than Windows 98.

'Would you like to come through?' the young woman says, taking your cup and pointing the way, and the moment you get in there you rattle through everything you want to say.

'This lady sent me a message alleging Declan Gray attacked her relative and they wanted to press charges. She named a police officer who took their complaint, but they released him that night because of no evidence. This was only a week before he killed Morgan . . .'

Nobody responds. But you can't stop. You worry that if you stop talking now, you'll never get chance to start again.

'Look, I don't know if it's true either,' you say. 'I just want it looking into properly. Couldn't you argue that the lad allegedly affected by this attack would be justified in carrying a knife now as the police did not help him when he asked for it? If this happened to him once, why should he ever trust the police again? Is this why young people carry knives?'

They all look at you. You realise nobody is taking minutes. It must be hard to know what to say to a grieving, angry father who wants to get to the truth. Like reasoning with a hungry bear. But shouldn't it be recorded? Won't that help things get done?

As the meeting ticks by, you can feel yourself losing the argument. Here you are with these four intelligent people trying to play them at their own game, when really you're just pissed off and getting on their tits. It's been two hours now, going over and over the same old points. You're almost out of words.

But not yet.

You lean across the table one final time, your skin tightening up, so they don't just hear what this means to you, they feel it as heat from your eyes.

'Tell me how bad you lot are going to look when Karlton Gray is released if he leaves prison with a manslaughter charge, as his brother did before he killed Morgan, and he reoffends,' you say. 'How bad will you look if this report is not done now?'

Neil doesn't sigh, but it feels as though he has.

'What kind of report do you want done?' he says, with a tone you feel is condescending. But don't lose your temper. Do what you came here to do. Show them who you are, Colin. Not someone who is scared by posh rooms full of intelligent people. Not someone who is going to give up.

'One like this,' you say, pulling a hefty bound document from your bag and tossing it on to the table, where it lands with a bang they hear back in reception.

The first you heard about Georgia Williams was when a comment appeared beneath your BBC interview on Facebook. It immediately jumped out from all the rest.

Don't be put off in what you are doing and don't give in. I know what it's like.

You clicked through to the profile of a woman named Lynnette. You messaged her straight away.

'What do you mean?'

The very next day you were talking on the phone, and she was telling you her story. And it wasn't easy to hear, because in her voice you heard suffering. In her voice you heard you.

THE MURDER OF GEORGIA WILLIAMS

Georgia Williams, of Wellington, Shropshire, had a life fuller than most seventeen-year-olds could comprehend. She was head girl at Ercall Wood Technology College, a member of the student council at New College, a corporal with the 1130 Wrekin Squadron Air Training Corps, a volunteer with AFC Telford United's match-day safety team and looking forward to a career in the Royal Air Force. She was described as 'everything you could want in a friend'.

On 26 May 2013 she was invited by a young man she knew, twenty-three-year-old Jamie Reynolds, to take part in a photo shoot at his parents' house while they were on holiday in Italy. She liked photography. She enjoyed helping people out. And so she agreed.

Reynolds hanged Georgia from a length of rope attached to the loft hatch until she was dead. He then posed her body, both partially clothed and naked, in different parts of the house, including on his parents' bed, while carrying out a series of sex acts that Georgia's father, Steven Williams, a serving detective with West Mercia Police, described in his Victim Personal Statement as 'horrific and beyond comprehension'.

During Reynolds's trial for Georgia's murder, Prosecutor David Crigman QC said Reynolds carried out a 'scripted, sadistic and sexually motivated murder', and that he had planned the killing meticulously. He'd bought items including a rope, a leather jacket, leather shorts and high heels for Georgia to wear. He'd taught himself how to tie a noose, and then how to attach it to a 'hanging mechanism'. When police later searched his home, they found a series of photographs he'd taken documenting her murder.

After using Georgia's phone to text her mother, Lynnette, telling her that Georgia was staying with friends, Reynolds loaded Georgia's body into his stepfather's van. He went to the cinema to watch a film in Wrexham, then dumped Georgia in woodland in the nearby Nant-y-Garth Pass, before driving to Glasgow, where, after a manhunt, he was arrested three days later. Georgia's body would not be discovered until five days after her disappearance.

Everything Reynolds did was wicked beyond belief.

Mr Crigman described Reynolds as a manipulative individual and 'a sexual deviant' who'd had 'a morbid fascination in pornography depicting violence towards women in a sexual context since at least 2008'. At the time of his arrest he had 16,800 images and seventy-two videos of extreme pornography stored on an external hard drive. These included digitally doctored images of up to eight women Reynolds personally knew, in which ropes had been added round their necks. He seemed to have been especially obsessed with red-haired women, like Georgia. Additionally, he'd written forty graphic short stories about women being murdered, then sexually violated. One was called 'Georgia Williams in Surprise', in which she died following a sex game. He'd also written a script about the trapping and killing of a victim, which appeared to have been carefully followed when he lured Georgia to his house.

On reading reports from psychiatrists, Justice Wilkie said: 'I take very seriously the conclusion of Professor Paul Peckitt that you have the potential to become a serial killer.' He sentenced Reynolds to a whole-life order, meaning he will never be released.

After sentencing, West Mercia Police's investigating officer, Detective Chief Inspector Neil Jamieson, said that Reynolds was 'a sadistic, and very dangerous, manipulative individual who preys on young females'. He also confirmed that a MAPPA Discretionary Serious Case Review was now under way, investigating the force's prior contact with Reynolds, because Reynolds, it transpired, was known to be dangerous before.

That review was published on 14 October 2015. It found that both the police and social services missed opportunities with regard to the danger Reynolds posed to others. The review concluded: 'The confused and uncoordinated approach to the case meant there was an element of misinformation operating between the agencies,' adding that work appeared to take place in 'silos'.

The opportunities police missed to identify Reynolds as a danger to young women were many and horrifying. In 2008 he had trapped another seventeen-year-old girl in his home, just as he later did Georgia, and tried to strangle her. But he wasn't prosecuted. Within two weeks of this horrific incident police were made aware that Reynolds had altered photos of local girls in a disturbing way, but the girls were not informed and no action was taken. After that there were a few years during which Reynolds didn't appear on the police's radar again, until 2011, when he was reported for reversing his car into that of a girl who rejected his advances. Police treated it as a traffic accident, as though he'd absent-mindedly hit a wall outside the supermarket, or accidentally run over his neighbour's foot, and not another unnerving incident in a pattern of mounting threat to any young woman unfortunate enough to enter his orbit.

After the MAPPA Discretionary Serious Case Review was published, a number of agencies jointly admitted a series of failures. West Mercia Police said they could and should have investigated Reynolds's previous behaviour in more detail, with Chief Constable David Shaw telling BBC News:

'We will make sure we're learning everything we can from this mistake, and others from other forces and other agencies. I can absolutely guarantee that this has been a shock to our organisation.'

Then Prime Minister David Cameron reiterated this emphasis on reflection, telling the House of Commons:

'What matters now is that police and the other agencies really study this report, and learn the lessons so that these mistakes aren't made again in future.' 'Learn the lessons' had by then become a catch-all term used frequently in the wake of institutional failure, so common, and with so little tangible change attached to it, that it rendered the words meaningless.

Covering the publication of the review, the BBC's Sian Lloyd said that the BBC had obtained another report into how the West Mercia Police Force investigated Reynolds, this one carried out by Devon and Cornwall Police. It named individual officers involved, and recommended disciplinary proceedings against some of them. One received a written warning. Two more received 'management advice'. Lloyd discussed these findings, and the MAPPA report, with Steven and Lynnette Williams on camera, the two grieving parents doing a commendable job of controlling an anger simmering just beneath the surface of an insurmountable grief:

'Over and above the fact that we have to live with Georgia being murdered in a terrible way,' Steven said, his face wrought with anguish, 'is, every day, what if, what if, what if, what if. They should have. They should have. They should have. Of course, that's what this is about. The police should have done things they didn't do. And that will be on my mind until the day I die.'

'You want all the facts out there,' Lynnette said. 'You want all the findings, you want the reports released.'

Though they had the report in their hands, in their eyes was a sense that this was not the end for them. That there could never be one.

Monday, 12 February 2018 (continued)

Neil picks up the MAPPA Discretionary Serious Case Review into the missed opportunities in Jamie Reynolds's past that Lynnette Williams kindly sent to you.

'When I asked Adrian McGee for a MAPPA Discretionary Serious Case Review,' you say, 'I was told that because Declan Gray was not on MAPPA after his release, we could not have one done.' You bring your finger down on the report. 'Jamie Reynolds was not on MAPPA either, but he got one. So why do the Williams family get one, and not us?'

'It's not the same,' Neil says. But you won't settle for that.

'Is it because Steven Williams was a police officer and knew how the system worked?'

In your head you've fantasised about them agreeing on the spot to a MAPPA Discretionary Serious Case Review into the possible mishandling of Declan Gray. You've thought of the tall, cold beer you'll have to celebrate.

But you don't get this moment. Instead, and before you can really take in what's happening, they're saying a MAPPA report isn't possible in your case. Then, just like that, the meeting is over, and you're shaking hands, and you're back outside on the pavement where the cold air turns your breath to smoke.

But you won't take no for an answer. You've one last thing to try. One last shot from the school of stubborn bastards. You email Marcus Jones, your MP, and you tell him everything you told Neil. And maybe your desire for the truth burns through the words, maybe his screen catches light with your rage, because in two days' time he replies saying he is in agreement, and that he has spoken to the Office of the Police and Crime Commissioner, and they've agreed a report will be done.

You did that. No one else. You did that. You.

A CONVERSATION WITH THE DOCTOR
WHO TRIED TO SAVE MORGAN'S LIFE

It took a long time to track down the doctors who treated Morgan on the night he died, and all the while you were trying – emailing the hospital, being passed from person to person – you were never quite sure whether it was a good idea. The thought of going through the details of exactly what happened in Intensive Care makes you feel sick. But Sue wants to know, and with time you've come to see it from her perspective. Never more so than when you hear those mindless, throwaway things people say to the mourning relatives of those who have passed too soon, like 'He is in a better place' and 'Maybe it's for the best' suggesting it's preferable that Morgan died than live with brain damage from the oxygen starvation, or something incomprehensible like that. How are you meant to envision another version of hell to the one you already inhabit? How are you supposed to think of Morgan alive, but in a different way? Maybe talking to the doctors can close those doors in your imagination. Maybe that's what Sue needs to do.

Eventually the hospital agrees to your request, and though you leave extra-early so the journey is calm, you end up spending ages looking for a parking space, which in Coventry could be classed as a high-stress extreme sport, so when you finally run through the doors of the hospital you're sweaty and entirely unprofessional in appearance. Which is no help to Dr Billyard, a friendly if confused-looking man, who shakes your hand as he admits, 'I'm not sure what this meeting is going to be about.'

You tell him you don't want to know in detail about the medical side of things – God forbid – but that it's important to Sue to sit with him now, and hear what happened that night. He agrees you shouldn't go through the files. It would be too much. But then he leads you to a private room that looks more like a classroom in a modern school than any part of a working hospital, and tells you to ask him any questions you want, he'll be happy to answer if he can. And so you hold Sue's hand, and that's exactly what you do.

'What happened when Morgan arrived at the hospital?' you ask.

Dr Billyard takes a second to recall, and you can see in his eyes that he's replaying the scene in his mind. The alarms. The urgency. The chaos.

'In theatre they managed to repair the damage to his heart and lung,' he says. 'Morgan was given fifty units of blood, which is five times the amount the human body needs. He would not stop bleeding out, the blood would not clot and it was coming from his kidney, which had been stabbed, and also the wound from the operation opening him up. They could not stop the bleeding. They had tried everything, using every known medicine.'

You nod, your appreciation plain even in your melancholy. What else can you do?

'Was there a point at which it was a blessing that Morgan died?' you say. 'Would he have suffered brain damage from a lack of oxygen, for instance?'

Dr Billyard shakes his head.

'No, if he had stopped bleeding he could have made a recovery. We tried everything we could and he was unlucky.'

Sue leans forward then. There is something she has always wondered, and in the loosening of her grip on your fingers you feel her relief at finally getting to say it aloud.

'Did you know Morgan was a colleague from the hospital?'

'Yes,' Dr Billyard says. 'We were aware. It was a really tough night for the medical team as they are not used to dealing with this kind of incident.'

'In court,' you say, 'the defence were trying to say Morgan hit the ground so hard on his head when he fell that it caused his heart to stop beating. Was there any truth in this?'

'Definitely not. No way,' Dr Billyard says, and it feels like a release to hear it from a man like him, who was there with your son and cared for him as best he could. To prove wrong the ghoulish defence they laid out in bad faith at the court. 'He was stabbed in the heart and other organs. There is not a chance his death was caused by a fall.'

Afterwards you stay and chat for twenty minutes about Morgan, the things being done in his name and an exhibition of his art you're planning. Then you thank the doctor for his time and he goes back to work, two swinging doors sweeping him back into the busy river of people rushing down the hospital corridor.

All days are difficult. But the days you hear truth from the mouths of good men are better than others.

Tuesday, 15 May 2018

You're a nuisance, Colin Hehir. And right now that's exactly what you want to be.

As you and Sue are ushered into a side room at Nuneaton Justice Centre (more biscuits on the table, her presence quelling those hops in your heart), it hits you that the police think you're a nuisance now too. It's unsaid as the two men greet you, but there's a sense that you know and they know you won't go away. You made your MP badger the Police and Crime Commissioner, and now it's fallen in their laps. You want a MAPPA Discretionary Serious Case Review done into Morgan's murder. And you won't stop asking until you get one.

The first man is one you've met before, Andy Wade, head of Probation, from the big MAPPA meeting. The second is new, the next card in a shuffling pack of faces. Assistant Chief Constable Richard Moore is tall, slim and handsome, you suppose, with a melodic Northern Irish accent. He's polite, smart and doing his best to put you at ease, even though he can see you're not the biggest fans of Warwickshire Police Force. He does that thing people do, where they say they have a son too, and how they cannot imagine what you're going through. It's not his fault, but you still find it difficult to hear. You just don't need it to be said, because it's obvious. Grief this deep is an unimaginable state of being. Sue is getting agitated too. Though her mouth doesn't move, she tells you so, in your head, loud and clear.

Before you get down to business, something has been bugging you. Sometimes it pops into your head while you're driving, and you stop concentrating on the road. Sometimes it's while you're eating, and you cease chewing for so long the food becomes mulch in your mouth. Sometimes it's while you're talking, and you realise too late there is silence, someone looking into your eyes, wondering where you have gone.

Before you get to the report, you need to tell Assistant Chief Constable Moore about it, to get it off your chest. About the night Morgan died. Because even Doctor Billyard who treated him in hospital mentioned it when you spoke, that the medical team thought the police were very heavy-handed and couldn't understand why they wouldn't let you see your son.

'Was it right that the policeman who turned up wouldn't let us see Morgan?' you ask.

Assistant Chief Constable Moore looks shocked. He takes a moment, so you fill the silence.

'I was threatened with being arrested if I insisted on wanting to see Morgan, even though the nurse had said they would get him ready for us.'

He shifts in his seat and sighs. This is clearly all news to him.

'It was how the officer interpreted the law,' he says, 'but no. He could have let you see your son.'

If you're ever asked whether you believe God exists, you won't answer yes or no. Instead you'll describe this feeling. It can't be possible to feel this low if there is a God. He wouldn't allow it.

That's when Assistant Chief Constable Moore hits you with it.

'A MAPPA Discretionary Serious Case Review is not what I believe should be done,' he says. 'I know you have seen the Jamie Reynolds Discretionary Report, but I do not believe it is appropriate in your situation.'

Sue bristles. She's got her take-no-bullshit head on, and you're absolutely fine with that.

'Why not?'

'Because no other agencies were involved in the monitoring of Declan Gray.'

The fury is so heavy in your head that it drops.

'I knew you would feel this,' he says. 'And I also know you probably feel that the Williams family got special treatment because Georgia's father is a police officer. But I will give you a report. An Overarching Case Review. It will be honest, and you will get the truth from these records we have here.' Under his hand are three substantial folders. Inside them is all the paperwork the police have on their past interactions with Declan Gray. 'We are not hiding anything, this report will be done and you will get a copy for you to do as you please with once it's complete.'

You can tell Sue wants to argue about it not being a MAPPA Discretionary Serious Case Review. But you? You're still deep inside yourself, back in time, at the hospital, not being allowed through the swing doors to see your boy. And you tell her without speaking:

We have to trust what he says, that he's going to be honest with us, because what else can we do?

And because she loves you, because she looks into your eyes and knows there is no fight left, she agrees. She'll drop it. She'll drop it for now. Even though she doesn't think she should. She doesn't think that this is enough. She doesn't believe that you're done. Not yet.

Astonishing, isn't it? That you can go through what you've been through, that you can have everything you thought you knew about yourself and the world bent and reshaped and pulled apart, but still you haven't learned the simple lesson that's been in front of you all this time. Sue is always right.

Friday, 22 June 2018

His face. Eamon's face when the Ferrari pulls up outside, all red and gleaming, the door opening like something from a film. This might be a nicer part of Nuneaton, but even here you wouldn't park that bugger without expecting someone to at least have away with the wheels.

'It's for you,' you say, and he doesn't quite believe it.

'You what?'

'It's for you. For your prom.' He squirms a bit, uncomfortable in his suit, but bloody hell he looks handsome.

'But,' he says, 'I don't deserve it.'

'Oh,' you say, 'but you do.'

It was Morgan's friend Cooper who tipped you off that there was a local businessman named Danny putting word around that he'd give the most deserving child a lift to the school prom in his Ferrari. And you couldn't think of anyone more deserving than Eamon. Not with how well he did in his GCSEs. Despite everything he's been through, he's not once gone off the rails, not once kicked back, not once turned to drugs, not once complained about the rough deal he's had. He's on track to succeed in life, where others might have withered. You say this to one of his teachers one day, thinking of Eamon getting into the Ferrari with a big smile on his face like he's Bruce bloody Wayne or something.

'I'm so happy for him, so happy for Eamon, considering what he's gone through,' you say. But the teacher just stares back blankly.

The phone rings later. The party is still going on in the background, and Eamon has clearly had a fair few drinks, but you don't mind a bit.

'I love you,' he says. 'And I love Mum too. And even Connor, I fucking love him too.'

'We know Eamon,' you say, 'we know.'

'And Morgan. I miss him. I wish you were happy. I fucking love you all.'

Saturday, 4 August 2018

Thousands of voices, all singing:

Summer's gone, winter's in your eyes
I can feel the thunder storms inside
I wake every morning and the cold winds cover me
All I've got's a ghost of what could be
If you can see the lights shine in front of me
If you can see the lights shout out where you'll be

At an outdoor concert in summertime, you feel like you used to feel. Only for a second, fleeting as a pinprick. But you feel it. With your best friends Tam and Helen beside you, your arms round Sue and a beer in your hand, good music, warm weather, that old sunshine in your belly. You love this. This is you.

There's no escaping middle age though, is there? Look around you. Simple Minds on stage. Simple bloody Minds! Stalls selling Pimm's. A queue for the toilet that must take half an hour to get through. You look at Sue, Tam and Helen, who've been so good to you, at your side through your dark moods, all your craziness, singing along at the tops of their voices, and wonder what you might have said back when you first met if you'd known the paths your life would go down to bring you to this point, where joy is just an echo from the past.

This is the song that gets you, though. The one that burrows into your heart. It feels as though it was written just for you, its lyrics whittled from your life:

Summer's gone, winter's in your eyes
I can feel the thunder storms inside

You think of Sue. You think of Morgan. And you sing.

If you can see the lights shout out where you'll be

Friday, 10 August 2018

It's here.

Assistant Chief Constable Moore sits beside Andy Wade. Tucked beneath his arm is the Overarching Case Review. Inside it, at last, is the truth you've been seeking. You want to leap across the table and grab it, but instead you wait for permission, like a well-trained dog with a snack perched on its nose. All while he tells Sue and you: it's a very thorough report, it's an honest one, it's very detailed – all the things someone might say about a report they've written. And because of this, the police have a duty to protect the victims. So you can read the report, but you cannot take notes, or photos, or copy any of it down. You cannot take it away with you. It is not yours.

And you think: but that's not what he said at the last meeting. He said you could have a copy to take away and do as you please. This is your report. It was done for you. You've no interest in tracking down the victims. You *are* the fucking victim.

But you don't say any of this, because there it is in front of you. The truth. And these last few minutes of waiting flay your skin from your bones. So instead you say the only words you can find that might make this happen sooner.

'OK. Let's see it then.'

Assistant Chief Constable Moore passes a copy of the report across the table for you and Sue to share. Not immediately, but in a minute or two you'll look up and see he and Andy have a copy each. And you'll never forget that.

But you focus on the copy in front of you, and as Sue flicks through the pages, you slowly realise exactly what its contents actually mean.

The police weren't lying about Declan Gray's offending when they admitted he'd been arrested while out on licence for his manslaughter charge, and three times between his release and killing Morgan.

But it's not the whole truth.

The whole truth is that the scale of Declan Gray's alleged offending was so vast and prolific, it seems the police did not know what to do with it. And if Declan Gray had been convicted of any of these offences, it's highly possible he would not have been standing on the balcony of a Nuneaton flat on 31 October 2015, as Morgan and his friends walked by. There are so many allegations, an embarrassment of alleged offending, that there is an actual list of it. There is intelligence that he was dealing heroin and crack cocaine, including while he was out on licence for manslaughter. While an offender is on licence, only suspicion is needed to recall them to prison. There is also a positive drug test while out on licence for manslaughter. Declan Gray disputed the finding so another test was done, but the results were lost.

There is a report of an alleged rape during the period when Declan Gray was out of prison on licence in which a witness said she saw Declan Gray pulling up his trousers and the alleged victim with a terrified look on her face, and him then threatening the alleged victim with retaliation if she pressed charges.

There is an allegation that while out on licence for man-slaughter, Declan Gray committed an aggravated burglary, entering a flat with a baseball bat to steal money and drugs and attacking two women, one of whom leaped from a first-floor window to escape. He was recalled to prison for this alleged aggravated burglary, but no one ever pressed charges and he was never charged with the crime.

There is an allegation that after his release from prison for manslaughter, he attacked someone with pool balls in a sock, for which he was arrested, but no one pressed charges and he was released without charge.

There is an allegation that after his release from prison he threatened someone with a knife, but again, no one pressed charges, though in this instance the Facebook message you received seemed to confirm someone wanted to.

Sue gently closes the report and lays it back on the table. It is quiet. What are you meant to do now? Go home, make a pot of tea, sit back and thank God it's over? Are you meant to just stop?

Assistant Chief Constable Moore tells you you'll get a redacted version of the report. But all you can think about is a YouTube clip of Georgia's father you saw late one night, when you couldn't sleep and were trawling the internet for anything that reflected your sorrow. In it, he was waving the redacted report he and his wife received and saying: 'This is like reading a novel but the ending is not there. The real report made us weep.'

'I don't see any accountability here,' you say. And it's true. This report is simply a list of things Declan Gray was accused of that the police knew about. It doesn't say *why* nothing happened. It doesn't show *how* nothing happened. It doesn't point the finger of blame at anyone, or anything. It's just a list. A catalogue of allegations, crimes and misdemeanours. It's a big 'fuck off and stop making a nuisance of yourself now', is all it is.

Assistant Chief Constable Moore, he's a nice guy. But he looks at you and doesn't say a word.

Tuesday, 18 September 2018

You've a phone in your hand and a head full of thunder. Where this goes, heaven knows. But you want everybody to know how you feel, because this much is now clear. Declan Gray was a danger, Declan Gray was a threat. *Declan Gray slipped through the net.* There were plenty of chances he could have been taken off the streets by Warwickshire Police, but they were not seized. The way you see it, Warwickshire Police are culpable for the death of your son.

The officer at the Police Professional Standards Department listens intently while you tell him the nature of your complaint against Detective Superintendent Adrian McGee. It's nothing personal, you say. It seems important to stress this, because Detective Superintendent Adrian McGee died suddenly last June. Flags were flown at half-mast out of respect, and the Chief Constable for Warwickshire Police, Martin Jelley QPM, said:

'Adrian was a hugely popular and highly respected police officer across his home force Warwickshire, our alliance partners West Mercia Police, and nationally in policing. He had the reputation of being both a very skilled and capable police officer but also a thoroughly decent, kind and genuine man by all who knew and worked with him.'

And you agree with every word of that. But the basis of your complaint is that you believe he was told by his superiors to fudge the questions you asked him about Declan Gray's supervision post-release. That's why they wanted them in writing, and that's why they took so long to return their responses to you. To make it easier to toss you some half-truths. To tell you just enough to make you go away. To repeat the same empty answers until you stopped asking the same questions. It's right there, isn't it, in the clip of you interviewing him on BBC News. He almost apologises, before the Police and Crime Commissioner says he already knows the police have done no wrong.

You don't think Detective Superintendent McGee had anything to gain personally from not telling you everything. You believe he was acting on orders from above because there was more to the story that would reflect badly on the police. Your complaint against Detective Superintendent McGee is therefore a complaint against the police itself. And so you want to make it.

You hear the tip-tapping of a keyboard. OK, the officer says, he'll get that processed and you'll hear back soon. But you've not finished. You also want to lodge a complaint against the Chief Constable.

'He is in charge,' you say. 'I hold him responsible. The buck stops with him.'

There is silence on the other end of the phone as the nice officer tries to be sure he isn't imagining everything you just said.

'Let me get this straight,' he says. 'You want to put in an official complaint against Adrian McGee for telling untruths, *and also* a complaint against the Chief Constable for the action of the force?'

'Yes,' you say, smiling for the first time in weeks. 'That's right.' You've this image in your head of the nice officer holding the phone out so everyone else in the office can hear it. Like it's just his luck to have answered to a loon. Some nutter firing off complaints left, right and centre about any old cop he can name. Who's next? Kojak? Columbo? Hercule bloody Poirot? He comes back a few minutes later to tell you that if you want to complain about the Chief Constable, you need to contact the Police and Crime Commissioner, Philip Seccombe, because only he has the power to discipline him.

All right. The Police and Crime Commissioner it is then. You email his secretary directly, because you're way past giving a shit, and you make it plain that you want Philip Seccombe to read a copy of the Overarching Case Review, and then to sack the Chief Constable.

And while you're at it . . . it's you who got this report done when the Police and Crime Commissioner didn't want to help, and now it's done you're not going to let him sit behind his desk and do nothing. So you fire off a third complaint, this one against the Police and Crime Commissioner himself for his failure to act. Three complaints. A hat-trick. A trio of thorns in the foot of a lion.

Your friend Dale sips his beer and listens while you unload on him about everything. The fight you're going through. The uncertainty about how it will all turn out that twists your insides at night. The loss of faith that you'll ever wring the whole truth from the system, that anybody will ever hold their hands up and admit to a mistake. And your determination to do it all for Morgan, because that's what this is about, and has been from the beginning.

He considers it for a good long while.

'You know,' he says, 'you're like a modern-day Don Quixote.' He's clever, is Dale. Great in a pub quiz. You nod and laugh a little, but you're only pretending you know what the hell he's talking about it. It's not until later, when you get home and Google it, that you laugh so hard your belly hurts.

Don Quixote was a delusional middle-aged Spanish man who was on a quest, re-enacting the chivalry of knights-errant and generally making a total arse of himself, until it seemed a lot like he had lost his wits.

And maybe that is you. Maybe he's right. Colin Hehir, with a sword in his hands, charging towards an enemy it's impossible to slay.

Wednesday, 7 November 2018

Maybe Assistant Chief Constable Moore and Andy Wade's handshakes aren't as firm this time. Maybe the coffee doesn't come as quickly, or it sat in the pot to stew too long. Maybe there are fewer biscuits on the table. You can't quite put your finger on why, but you can feel a change in the atmosphere the moment you enter Nuneaton Police Station. And you can see Assistant Chief Constable Moore's point when he tells you that all of your complaints have made it awkward. In fact, it's difficult to even have this meeting as protocol would dictate, because in effect your complaint against the police is a complaint against Assistant Chief Constable Moore himself. And he's right. It's very awkward indeed. It's like telling your grandma her apple pie tastes like it was found in a toilet and still going round there, expecting to be fed.

But you don't care. You're not flesh any more. You're metal. You whirr with apoplexy. And they hear it. Maybe that's why they tell you: the Overarching Case Review will no longer be redacted and given to you as promised. You will never get a copy. Not even one with all the meat cleaved from the bone.

You're about to explode out of your seat when the look on Assistant Chief Constable Moore's face tells you what's really going on here. This isn't about stopping you. Not this time. Not like every other time. This is because of you kicking up a fuss. Because of your complaints, questions are now being asked of the Overarching Case Review itself on a much higher level. And the MAPPA meeting you attended at the behest of the Police and Crime Commissioner – the one where no minutes were taken – is being scrutinised too. Assistant Chief Constable Moore underlines it: this might have an impact at a national level.

What you've done has put the police on the back foot. Which begs the question: what was missing from the Overarching Case Review? What mistakes were made that weren't reported in it? And who was it protecting?

There was more to the story. You knew it. You bloody knew it. And when you close your eyes, you see Morgan spinning away from the bulging goal, lifting his shirt to reveal the message scrawled across his vest.

Tuesday, 2 November 2018

Jimmy's sleeping peacefully on the rug, his legs pumping through dreams of something better, and you're jealous.

Being unconscious has been your only respite this week, what with Halloween and the third anniversary of Morgan's death. This time round your PTSD got so bad you had flashbacks. Work kindly moved you to a better duty, just shifting loads from depot to depot, so you wouldn't run into a plastic pumpkin or a Frankenstein mask, or your worst fear – the one that hurts the very core of you – a priest costume. But this time of year the scar turns soft again wherever you are, whatever you're doing. It tears, the wound opens up, and sleep is the only time you forget.

The dog wakes up when the phone rings. It's Sue's sister Marie, and it takes a while for Jimmy to stop yapping before you can really get to grips with what she's trying to tell you.

Oh no.

You take Sue and you hold her. It is so familiar, to be entwined by grief.

Sue's dad, Peter, died in hospital on 31 October at 9 p.m., almost exactly three years since Morgan was killed. He'd survived strokes, and though he was well into his eighties, of late he'd been a shell of his former self. But he'd lived life exactly how he'd wanted to, taking no nonsense from anyone, a virtue clearly in his genes.

Marie had handled it well. She knew Sue wouldn't be able to take the news on the anniversary of Morgan's passing, so she'd waited a few days, and for that you're both thankful.

You always liked Peter. He'd been a massive influence on you as a younger man, and it's only now you realise you owe him much of your fortitude. Or at least, he was to thank for bringing Sue into the world, someone who never took an ounce of your bullshit. Who dragged you through these last three years. You'll always be grateful for any part he played in creating someone capable of what seemed impossible.

But losing a parent is different to losing a child. To lose a parent is to put a frame round the past, hang it up on a wall and know the picture was complete. To lose a child is to live with a wall that won't be built.

A HOLIDAY IN ITALY SIX MONTHS FROM NOW

You'll feel different. It doesn't seem possible now. But you will.

One day, not too far away, Sue will book a holiday to Pisa for you both. For her fortieth you went to Rome, which was beautiful but a little too busy. Tuscany, however, is healing. At least according to Vincenzo, an old friend of yours, who should know. So it makes perfect sense. That's where you'll go.

From the moment you arrive you'll know you've made the right decision. The apartment is in the heart of Pisa, the leaning tower within walking distance, and across the street is Nonna's Café, which serves pizza so fresh and wine so cheap it tastes like bliss. You'll be surrounded by tall, elegant cypress trees that, as the light dips, look like paintbrushes against the canvas of the warm evening sky.

Later you'll notice the police riot vans lined up along the ancient city walls, then the whistling and shouting of a nearing crowd carrying flares. At first you'll be unsettled – Sue will down her wine like you should get out of here – but the waitress explains that the local Pisa football team have just won a cup final. Soon the atmosphere swallows you, all these happy young people giving you the high fives to which you were once allergic, asking where you're from and wrapping their arms round you in celebration of the game, the night, their lives.

You will think of your sons. Of Morgan. Of Eamon. Of Connor, who has moved out of home now, to Leeds, where he has a girlfriend and a job and is building a life for himself with the kind of independence that in one way or another he always sought. He's still doing what he loves most – making music – but the sound has morphed from when Morgan was in the band into something darker, from somewhere deeper within. They are no longer called Fade. Now they're called Mourning. And they've a song named 'Grut Forever', which is Connor's way of memorialising Morgan, you suppose. His way of getting it out. You'll be so proud of him.

And you'll think of your sons the next day, too, when you head away from the coachloads of tourists arriving at the Leaning Tower of Pisa towards the hidden side of the city. It's rough around the edges. The churches are empty ruins, the streets bend into darkened alleyways. Not so long ago you and Sue would have hated it here. You'd have been scared to venture this far from the main drag. But not now. Now you push open the church doors and find the ancient walls covered in graffiti. And it is glorious. Sue photographs it and you take turns to point out pieces that you like, in love with how the paint has given life to the crumbling bricks. Afterwards you'll hop between local bars full of Italian students, and it's so vibrant and urgent you'll feel completely alive, the energy of the city filling you up and making you anew. Maybe you'll even have a dance. Imagine that.

And you will stand, a bottle of Tuscan red wine beneath your arm, before the southern wall of the Church of Sant'-Antonio Abate, where in June 1989 Keith Haring created a 180-metre mural, *Tuttomondo*, one of his last public works before his death. You will see that it shows all mankind – the good, the troubled, the evil – jostling for space in pursuit of peace and harmony that doesn't come. An epic display of graffiti that encompasses all the world. Invigorated by the artwork, and thinking of the art your sons all made, you'll put your arm round Sue and smile at one another, not running away or going over old ground but accepting who you are, who you've come to be.

Monday, 18 February 2019

You can tell you've kicked up a stink, because these last few weeks it feels like all you've done is deal with people who are dealing with your complaints. There is a hurriedness to it, an energy that reminds you of someone trying to shoo away a wasp.

The woman charged with investigating your complaint into the Police and Crime Commissioner says she's found that he was unsure of what you really wanted after the MAPPA meeting. That he didn't know you wanted a review done. Well, that smells like horse shit to you. Reviews and inquiries were all you bloody talked about.

But it doesn't matter. They find that the complaint against the Police and Crime Commissioner is not substantiated. And, if you're honest with yourself, even in your wildest David and Goliath fantasies, that's kind of what you expected. The institution to fold around itself.

The same is true of your complaint into the Chief Constable, which is squashed before it's even found its feet.

But it's OK. It's OK. Because you get an email.

You made such a noise that Warwickshire Police referred your remaining complaint about the police to the Independent Office for Police Conduct (IOPC). Now they are conducting an investigation which will examine Warwickshire Police's dealings with Declan Gray in the weeks and months before he murdered Morgan.

You wonder if it's sunk in for the Police and Crime Commissioner that it all looks pretty bad, the fact that this IOPC report is happening because of your bloody-mindedness, not him pushing for a case review when he had the chance. But it's not a *Rocky* moment. You're not running up the steps of Philadelphia Museum of Art with your arms aloft. Because who knows? Maybe the IOPC report will show that Warwickshire Police did everything they could. If it does, you'll have to accept that. But you've stirred up a real shitstorm here. Because of you, a report will be done that will lay bare the events that proceeded Morgan's murder. And you will get what you and your family have wanted all along. The truth.

Monday, 18 March 2019

You miss your father's death.

When you arrive, your family are all there with him. He was not alone.

You loved him. And it hurts. But your pain is dwarfed by the pain that came before it. You can't find the words to explain that, so you don't say a thing but goodbye.

Thursday, 4 April 2019

You lay the envelope on the kitchen table and stare at it. You knew the IOPC report was going to come today. The police emailed you at 8.30 a.m. to inform you as much. But that hasn't made opening the envelope any easier. Are you nervous? Worried? Anxious this won't go your way? Or is it because this might finally be over?

You make a cup of tea and then you slide your index finger beneath the flap of the envelope. The cheap glue splits, and the thirty-two-page report flops on to the table like entrails. A final deep breath, then you scan the opening page, which suddenly seems to purge itself of meaning, leaving you looking for anything (a word, just a word) to cling to. A word to tell you how this ends.

And there it is.

Upheld.

Is that?

Does that mean?

You Google it to be sure.

UPHOLD

verb

past tense: **upheld**; past participle: **upheld**

confirm or support (something which has been questioned).

What it means is that you were right. There was so much you didn't know. Until now.

A TRAGEDY IN NUNEATON: PART FOUR
THE MISHANDLING OF DECLAN GRAY

THE CUE BALL

Everything about the day was new, and anything could still be made of it, when Declan Gray walked out of Her Majesty's Prison Glen Parva on Tuesday, 16 June 2015. Earlier that morning he'd completed his sentence for manslaughter, committed when he was aged just fifteen. Having entered these walls as a boy, he was leaving as a man. But he would be in trouble again before the moon was up.

It was 8.14 p.m. that evening when Warwickshire Police control room received a call from a person who wished to remain anonymous. The incident log described a scene of explosive violence:

> Declan Gray has just got out of prison and is going around knocking people out. He has punched someone in the face and knocked them out. The victim is on the floor and still breathing. Declan is with his mother and is fighting. Declan has been chased into the recreation ground. After knocking the victim out . . . he started on other people.

The police arrived at the scene quickly, but found nothing like the pandemonium that had been described on the phone. In fact, they reported back that the situation was 'all quiet'. From their initial inquiries, it appeared no one had seen or heard anything like what was recorded in the incident log, including the victim, who informed them he'd not been beaten up, but had in fact fallen over. The ambulance crew who examined him had no reason to disbelieve him either. They said the injury was consistent with a fall, possibly against the corner of a wall or similar. The victim's friend corroborated this, saying he thought the victim had slipped because he'd been drinking heavily. And anyway, neither of them had seen anyone around who might have caused an injury like this, so it must have been a drunken tumble. It can't have been anything else, otherwise surely someone would say, wouldn't they?

After that there wasn't much more the police could do. There was no sign of Declan Gray, no witnesses to his presence, and even his alleged victim said no crime had been committed.

Until the next morning.

Having spent the night in hospital getting the four-inch gash in his head glued back together, the victim contacted the police again to report that he had in fact been attacked by Declan Gray after all.

'Because I was knocked out,' he said by way of explanation, 'I did not know I'd been assaulted.' When the police visited him later, his statement was entirely different from the story he'd drunkenly told them the night before while an ambulance team patched up his wound. He now alleged he'd been talking to his neighbours when Gray approached, accusing him of mouthing off at Gray's mother following an incident involving the theft of some tobacco a few days earlier.

'Leave me alone,' the victim said. 'All I've done is get my bacca back. I don't need the trouble.' The victim then alleged that he turned to leave and was hit over the head two or three times before falling unconscious. This, of course, was as much as he remembered.

That same evening, an informant called the police claiming to have information about the assault. The weapon, they said, was a cue ball, taken from a pool table and wrapped in a sock, and it could be found in a wheelie bin next to where the attack took place. Sure enough, investigating officers found a ball in the bin, but no sock. The detective constable forwarded the ball to forensics for examination, then followed that up with an email. But the email didn't mention the fact there was a witness who could put Gray at the scene, nor that they'd described the ball as a weapon. Actually, it lacked any key information that might have enabled those charged with examining the ball to make a fully informed decision. It was signed off with:

'We appreciate this is a long shot but at least we have asked the question,' which suggested no thought had been given to any DNA or fingerprints that might be found on the ball. This would have been a golden opportunity to gather potential evidence. The forensic investigator later confirmed that the ball would not be forensically examined because 'This item is a moveable object and it cannot be linked to the crime and any DNA from the victim is likely to be found on the sock.' And 'If the ball was in the sock then any transfer from the victim would be in the sock. While you could fingerprint the pool ball, this could potentially give you a suspect's fingerprints, but without being able to link it back to your victim I don't really see the point.'

And even though forensic examination of the ball could have provided a valuable link between Gray, the alleged weapon and the victim, that was that.

Gray was arrested on 22 June, replying to being cautioned with the words, 'Are you sure it's not my brother?'

In his interview he gave a full account of his whereabouts after leaving prison that morning. He'd headed straight from HMP Glen Parva in Leicestershire to Nuneaton, where he was met by his girlfriend. He ate at McDonald's, then went to the George Eliot pub in Nuneaton town centre, and then The Crew, a bar on the outskirts of the town centre, where he hung out for a couple of hours playing pool.

Later he met his mother, who insisted he meet some of her friends in a flat close to Pool Bank Recreation Park. After staying there for about forty minutes he met a friend, another person, and his brother. While there he noticed some Asian men were congregating in the area, so he left, because he claimed to have had problems with them in the past. He denied any knowledge of an assault and stated once again that his brother looked just like him. That this might all be a case of mistaken identity. And while that seemed unlikely, it was not impossible. Karlton and Declan did look similar, at least from distance. They had short hair, round eyes and squat, muscular frames. They shared the gait of people who'd move unflinchingly towards trouble. Squint and they could be twins.

While Gray was in custody, officers went out into the community with the intention of obtaining statements and gathering evidence to assist in building a case strong enough to have him remanded there. They were met not just with silence, but with fear.

One person began to give an account of what happened, before refusing to make a statement because a rumour was going around the area that anyone providing a statement to the police would have their house firebombed or their windows put in. Another refused to provide a statement, even though they had been the one to make the initial anonymous call to police. In the interim they'd changed their mind, though it was unknown whether this was linked to what somebody else told the officers – that locals were 'shit-scared' to give statements.

Reluctance to talk was not the only issue. Someone who saw at least some of the incident didn't have their statement taken because it would have required an interpreter. And the same person who'd initially informed the police a pool ball was used in the assault wrote to Nuneaton and Bedworth Borough Council with third-party information regarding the assault and then apparently vanished. It was recorded that they no longer lived at their old address, and they failed to respond to attempts to communicate via email. But despite the importance of the person to the case – given they'd flagged the pool ball's location – no officers contacted the High Tech Crime Unit regarding the feasibility of obtaining the identity or location of this person via their mobile phone number. They may have tried to disappear, but they were never sought.

Despite the officers involved in the investigation being aware of the danger Gray posed and the fact he had been released from prison for manslaughter that morning – aware enough that they actively looked for potential witnesses whose statements could keep him in custody – there was nothing to suggest anybody from the police contacted the Local Neighbourhood Team, who might have been able to put in place a strategy to allay the community's fears of reprisal and potentially secure a witness statement. Nor was the case kicked up the chain of command to a detective inspector or other senior investigating officer, as would have been apt considering Gray was a known violent offender.

Although Declan Gray stated that he'd been with his brother that night, not one officer approached Karlton Gray as a witness: he was not traced, interviewed or eliminated as a potential suspect. Neither was their mother contacted, despite Declan Gray saying he'd been with her, and the victim alleging she'd been present at the time of the assault.

With no one willing or able to link Declan Gray to the alleged attack, he was released on bail, and an officer on the case updated the investigation log with a distinct air of resignation:

I have a number of witnesses, however not one will give a statement. The injured party is fully aware and knows none of his mates [and/or] local residents will help him and he accepts this. There is nothing forensically that can be done. There is no CCTV. There is nothing I can go to CPS with. This does not pass the threshold test. Please file NFA.

NFA meant No Further Action. The officer had hit the end of the road.

It was easy to see why it might seem so hopeless. There *were* no witnesses on record, there *were* no forensics, and, crucially, there was no CCTV. An initial CCTV trawl had revealed that the local Domehawk CCTV system that covers the area of the alleged attack had been removed.

But there was also nothing to suggest that officers looked beyond these parameters, to nearby Pool Bank Recreation Ground for example, where any cameras between The Crew public house and the flats may have shown Gray approaching the scene in possession of a pool ball. Or it may have shown Gray fleeing the scene at speed, negating his account that nothing happened. Equally, there was nothing to suggest that officers made any attempt to obtain CCTV from The Crew itself, where Gray admitted to having spent a few hours playing pool. It would even have identified the clothing worn by Declan Gray on the day of the assault, which would have given the arresting officer the opportunity to search for and seize this clothing for forensic purposes, given that the victim bled heavily as a result of the attack. And there was no attempt made to take a statement from The Crew's landlord, who'd likely have known if a pool ball from the table in his pub was missing and when it might have disappeared. In fact, the whole investigation was peppered with mistakes and missed opportunities that, if taken, might have linked Gray to the attack and removed him from the streets.

But that's another timeline entirely. One where, on the evening of 31 October 2015, Morgan Hehir and five of his friends arrive at the bar of The Crew, order a round of beers, raise their glasses and drink to what the future holds.

THE THEFT

There were a number of people staying overnight in the house when £180 in cash and a Galaxy Tablet went missing on 13 September 2015. Declan Gray was just one of them.

When the victim called the police they responded quickly, gathering circumstantial evidence from two witnesses, but neither provided any proof that Gray was responsible for the theft. It was immediately clear that this wouldn't be an open-and-shut case, if there was a case at all, that is. The victim, although she'd provided a statement, told the investigating officer that she would not support the investigation and would not go to court. There were no forensic or CCTV opportunities, and no witnesses who saw the property being stolen. Not only that, there were a whole bunch of people sleeping over, each a potential suspect alongside Gray, none of whom could be ruled out, although the victim stated that she did not believe they would have been responsible because she knew them.

Gray was arrested and denied any involvement in the theft. And as there was no evidence, he was free to go. But there was nothing to suggest that any consideration had been given to searching for the stolen property at the address he gave as his own; and so, although this was not a violent offence and in all likelihood Gray would not have received a custodial sentence even if he had been found guilty of theft, it could never be said that everything had been done.

THE FEAR OR PROVOCATION OF VIOLENCE

The boy was travelling on a skateboard, and not yet the victim of something awful, when he fell off while turning a corner at 8.19 p.m. on Friday, 19 October 2015. Perhaps if he'd not fallen at that exact moment on that exact spot, he'd never have become a victim at all. But cruelty often works that way, an inverse serendipity.

From the ground, where he sat and picked grit from his knees, the boy spotted the offender across the street, who started hurling abuse about his skateboarding ability. They'd never laid eyes on one another before. The boy said he was still learning. The offender responded, 'I'll learn you,' and started throwing stones and spitting. 'I'll show you,' he said, 'with my Stanley blade. I'll cut you up. I'll slice you up.' It was then that the boy saw something in the offender's hand. A sharp object, undeniably a Stanley knife, just as he'd claimed. It can only have been there to do harm.

The woman who stuck her head out of the window of a nearby flat made a timely intervention.

'What are you doing?' she said to the offender. 'Get in.' The offender had something resembling a moment of clarity in the thick of his fury and did as he was told.

The boy called the police, and while waiting for them to arrive he watched the offender, who could be seen changing his clothes in the first-floor window of the woman's flat. When the police did arrive, the boy pointed the offender out to them and they went to investigate.

The flat's occupant let them in, where they found a number of men and women who all denied that anyone else had been in the premises – a truth they maintained even when the officers pointed out they'd already seen the offender with their own eyes in that very room, through the window. There was definitely someone else there, unless this had been a weird apparition. They all refused to assist the officers in any way, though the officers didn't record this in the crime report for the handover to the interviewing officers, as they should have done.

The officers searched, and quickly found the offender hiding behind the bathroom door. He was arrested and provided the name Karlton Gray. But when challenged by the officers, he gave his full and real name instead. His name was Declan Gray. He was searched, as was the room he'd been seen in, from which Gray fetched his trainers, but there was no sign of a Stanley knife anywhere.

Gray was interviewed the next day, and a summary of the interview recorded in the investigation log.

> He denied even leaving the flat and stated that he did not see anyone on a skateboard, nor was he verbally abusive to anyone on the evening of the offence. Declan denied knowing the victim, or either having, owning or ever being in possession of a Stanley knife.

Though Gray said he hadn't left the flat, one of the occupants let slip to an officer that Gray had been outside. This information wasn't recorded in the crime report, meaning Gray's alibi went unchallenged.

There was no record of what challenges, if any, were put to Gray over his version of events. It was unclear whether police made further inquiries to trace the potential witness who called Gray back to the house immediately after the alleged incident. It was not known if a subsequent visit was made to the flat where Gray was arrested in an attempt to corroborate his alibi, or whether house-to-house inquiries were carried out in an effort to trace potential witnesses, or whether a CCTV trawl was undertaken in the area, all despite Declan Gray being a known violent offender with a manslaughter conviction, plus a recent arrest for violent assault.

The matter was subsequently filed as undetected, though it was later accepted that the investigation could, potentially, have been sent to the CPS for advice, because CPS guidelines state that in such circumstances they do consider prosecution. Just as it was accepted that not all the relevant information was handed over to the officers who interviewed Gray, making that process wholly problematic, and that the investigation was concluded prematurely, as other feasible lines of investigation were still outstanding. Without tracing witnesses to support the victim's account, or potential CCTV footage that might have done the same, this matter was just one person's word against another's. Those two people were the boy – someone with no previous convictions whose statement was compelling, timely and featured aspects corroborated by police – and Declan Gray, a known violent offender, who changed his clothes after the offence, was found hiding behind a bathroom door to avoid arrest and who gave the name of his brother when he was caught.

A relative of the victim would later allege that they were not given a crime number, which meant that, when they called the non-emergency police number the next day, any desire they had to press charges came to nothing.

Had any of these opportunities been taken, and resulted in Declan Gray being in police custody twelve days later when a group of young men happened to walk past a balcony on Meadow Court, Morgan Hehir, in fancy dress and enjoying an evening out with his friends, would not have been murdered with a blade that makes a Stanley knife look like a child's toy.

The tea in the mug on your kitchen table is cold. Your skin, too.

Eleven police staff – officers, detectives, sergeants and a forensics officer – are named in the report. All of them were spoken to for the review, all of them accepting there were missed evidential opportunities across their three separate investigations. You read the conclusion to the review again, and again, and again, scrambling for a foothold in the words. This piece of paper that corroborates why Morgan is not here.

Read it. Go on. With fury in your eyes, read it again:

[All of the officers spoken to] during the three years that have since past have become more experienced and skilled in the area of investigation to a standard that is necessary to complete a full and proper investigation. All have agreed they will reflect on and learn from this experience. Although we will never know if any of these three investigations would have led to the prosecution of Declan Gray, it has provided the opportunity to learn from the missed opportunities. I am satisfied that all of the Police Officers have accepted that opportunities were missed and they understand the consequences of not making a full record of the actions they do complete.

But Morgan's murder was the consequence.

From an organisational learning perspective the outcome of this review will hopefully allow Warwickshire Police to assess and ensure that front line Police Officers have the appropriate investigative skills and knowledge around identifying evidential opportunities which also allow them to provide an expectable level of service to all victims.

But Morgan was the victim.

I consider it equally important that supervisors should be reminded that they are a safety net for the investigating officer and should also have the skills and knowledge to allow them to make a decision on whether or not there is justification to file a crime as undetected, or identify further actions that need to be carried out by the investigating officer.

But this was their job and it was not done.

Declan Gray was an extremely violent individual who was allowed back in the community following his release from prison and so consideration could/should have been given to a Single Point of Contact when Declan Gray became a suspect and so enabling the Police to focus on ensuring every effort was given to bringing him to justice.

But Declan Gray was a convicted, violent criminal. Every effort should already have been made to bring him to justice to protect those in the community.

It is clear that the identified lesson learning means that this complaint is upheld, however it does not mean that these findings would have changed the final outcome of the murder of Mr Hehir, or that this was due to any professional standards or codes of ethics being breached by the officers investigating these crimes.

But because of failing after failing after failing, Morgan is dead.

And that is all there is. No one is taking responsibility. The only repercussions for anyone involved were just a bunch of off-the-record conversations with cops about the past mistakes they're apparently better than now, because the buck will not stop. There is only a complaint that has been upheld.

You don't hold those eleven police officers responsible for Morgan's death. At least they arrested Declan Gray. Yes, they made mistakes. Terrible, life-changing, life-ending mistakes. Yes, they were incompetent and not fit for the job. But they, too, were failed. They were failed by those above them. Not a single one of their missed evidential opportunities was identified by their superiors, the supervisory officers who filed the investigations as 'undetected'. The jump was not only botched, the safety net was missing. They were failed by the agencies and procedures in place to keep people like you, like Morgan, safe. They were failed by the system they are a part of.

Declan Gray was also failed. He was failed by the agencies he'd been involved with for much of his young life. He left prison deemed safe to re-enter the community, and exit MAPPA, without a single shred of supervision, simply for completing his sentence for an exceptionally violent crime. There was no next stage of offender management, despite all the indicators that he would offend again. There was no one to stop what happened next. There was no net to catch him either, just a chain of mistakes that meant he was free to kill. But not a single individual has been held accountable. The force is as faceless as it is culpable. The system is as broken as your heart.

What did you think the truth would feel like? Warm, like sunshine on your face? Sweet, like sugar on your tongue? A release, like the lifting of a weight from your chest? It is none of these things. It is cold, sour and heavy. But it is OK. Losing a son has taught you not to long for a world where things go your way. That version of you ceased to exist one night in October, a few long, short years ago.

Friday, 5 April 2019

You grip the cold handle of the coffin firmly and lift it on to your shoulder. Connor and Eamon are behind and beside you. Its lightness bears no relation to the weight of this duty. To carry your father as he once carried you. To be a son.

You do everything you can not to cry. He was a good man, a loved man, with a big family, all here to share their memories of his long, full life. But it's easier for you to be at something sad than it is to pretend to be happy. The tears still come.

Thursday, 11 April 2019

You're high up in your truck, approaching the centre of Birmingham, where the grey towers rise like groynes from the sand. Close to Villa Park, you approach a traffic island. There's this sense you get sometimes, a gift truckers have, that there is something coming before you see it in your mirror. And when you glance across, there is. A car, moving at high speed, rounding you as it approaches the island too quickly, its driver unaware, or aware too late, that just beyond the island is a zebra crossing, and on the zebra crossing is a young man on a bike.

You're not sure which happens first: the driver of the car hitting the brakes, or the young man realising he's about to be struck and bracing for impact, but the screech of tyres on the road stretches the time between now and catastrophe.

It does not come to pass. The car stops inches from the terrified young man, who falls off his bike on to the road.

His face flashes quickly through shock, then relief, then fury. He leaps to his feet, checking himself over to be sure he's all there, then starts screaming at the occupants of the car, three of them, now winding down their windows and shouting back. The young man rears up, cricks his neck. He wants to fight. He doesn't care about being outnumbered. None of the drivers in the queue behind can see past your truck, which is blocking them now, and their horns build to an impatient rhythm. The young man nears the car and starts hammering on it with his fists.

'Come on!' he says, his face twisted. He wants damage. He wants revenge. Suddenly he reaches down into his jacket pocket. When his hand emerges, a blade glints in the sun.

The driver spots the knife a moment after you do. His foot hits the accelerator and the car lurches down the road and out of sight.

The young man has nowhere to direct his anger then, until he looks at you, high above him. His eyes are wide and round, his teeth bared and white. He comes towards you. The knife has given him an abominable confidence. An indomitable surety. As though he were the one in the safety of a cabin. He knows nothing of what can be done by a blade in a hand. What can be taken away, or what can be left behind. He knows nothing of what you have lost.

'What are you fucking looking at?' he says.

And without blinking, you raise your hand and point at him, your finger sharp and steady.

'You,' you say. 'You.'

He gets on his bike and is gone.

Friday, 9 August 2019

You know Nuneaton Justice Centre too well these days. Like the back of your hand. Like the basement of your heart. The smiling receptionists are familiar. Assistant Chief Constable Moore's handshake is familiar. The biscuits are familiar. There's a woody scent to dormant dust in corridors that will always make you think of this place now. Of waiting for answers that sometimes don't come. Of pushing for more.

Gut instinct. That's what you put it down to. Gut instinct that there was more you didn't know. Olivia told you right at the start of all this that you should always follow your gut, and she was right. You've amazed yourself. You'd never say that to anyone, of course. You're not a dickhead. But it's true.

Today you're here because the Strategic MAPPA Board have inspected the Overarching Case Review and the IOPC Review, both of which were only ever done because you never stopped asking, and they've drawn some conclusions of their own.

Assistant Chief Constable Moore ushers you and Sue into the meeting room. The table is covered in sandwiches and cakes. Quite a spread, like the Queen is due or something. He explains it's all leftovers from a previous meeting, but that you can tuck in, if you like. And then he smiles and says, 'This almost looks like we're trying to sweeten you up.'

Everybody laughs at that, even you.

243

There's a pause before you get down to business. In this room all pauses feel ominous. Assistant Chief Constable Moore hands you and Sue a letter, one each this time, just a couple of pages long. A summary of everything that's happened: the Overarching Case Review, which the police take credit for commissioning without acknowledging your fight for it, an apology that their investigations were not as thorough as they could have been, a reiteration that their findings show there were no breaches of standards of professional behaviour or code of ethics, and finally a list of ten improvements to offender management which the Strategic MAPPA Board recommend to help ensure that what happened to Morgan never happens again. Change, on a national level.

The letter ends, 'I do hope that the work you have seen provides reassurance that as professional public servants we are always seeking to improve to ensure the risks are minimised as far as possible.'

You take what you hope will be your final free biscuit, and when the meeting is done, Assistant Chief Constable Moore releases a statement which Claire Harrison publishes in full in the *Nuneaton News*:

The murder of Morgan Hehir was a horrific crime that shocked the local community. Our thoughts remain with his family as they continue to come to terms with his death. Declan Gray is clearly a violent and dangerous man and we have therefore completed a thorough review of police investigations into his previous alleged offending. We can't say that had the previous investigations been carried out to the highest standard it would have led to the earlier prosecution of Gray or subsequently changed what happened.

However, we have identified that some investigative opportunities may have been missed in the three investigations reviewed. For this, I have personally apologised to Morgan's family and wish to reiterate this apology publicly.

Following the review, which was carried out by our Professional Standards Department, there was no evidence to suggest that any of the officers involved in the investigations breached any standards of professional behaviour and since this time, they have all become more experienced and skilled. However, they have all been provided with appropriate advice and guidance about their performance at the relevant times.

It is important the local community has confidence in Warwickshire Police and I would like to reassure people that our processes for investigation and managing violent offenders in the community have developed considerably since Morgan's death.

We are committed to learning from the findings of this review and ensuring the necessary improvements are put in place. I will continue to work closely with the Hehir family to reassure them of the improvements we have made and will continue to make.

A follow-up statement from the Police and Crime Commissioner, Philip Seccombe, adds:

I have every sympathy for Mr Hehir and his family, who have had to deal with the loss of their son in horrific circumstances and have understandably been seeking to ensure that no other parents have to go through the same experience in the future. I too share that desire and since my first meeting with Mr Hehir I have been working to ensure that all agencies involved review their procedures and make suitable changes to reduce the chances of similar circumstances happening again.

I have been very clear to Mr Hehir from the outset that as Police and Crime Commissioner my role is to hold the Chief Constable to account and that I am prohibited from interfering with operational policing matters. I do not have any direct formal governance role in other criminal justice agencies nor am I able to pursue complaints against the police on behalf of residents.

However I have always sought to provide every support and encouragement possible to Mr Hehir as he has sought answers around the circumstances leading to Morgan's death. This has included putting him in touch with the appropriate individuals and agencies who can undertake case reviews.

I always seek to provide a link between the public and the police and to that end I raised Mr Hehir's concerns with the Chief Constable on a number of occasions. Recognising that the issues the case raises go beyond just policing, however, I also organised a meeting at which Mr Hehir and I were able to question senior representatives of the police, probation, youth justice, courts, legal experts and the prison service about the arrangements which are in place to protect the public in Warwickshire from dangerous offenders.

As a result of this meeting, a number of changes have been made to tighten processes between the criminal justice agencies in Warwickshire and additional training has been organised for frontline practitioners in the county.

I have also made significant extra resources available to the police during my term of office, which is enabling the recruitment of 150 additional police officers and staff into Warwickshire, including large numbers of additional officers involved in patrol policing and investigation, with an enhanced capability to manage prolific offenders.

I have been reassured that the changes in offender management that have been made since Morgan's death remain effective. However I am continuing to press the police and all of our criminal justice agencies to ensure that there is a continued focus on improvement.

This will ensure that the public can remain confident that all that can be done to keep people safe from dangerous individuals in Warwickshire is being done.

You and Sue sit in the car outside the Justice Centre, hearing but not listening to the low hum of the ring road. She doesn't reach over from the passenger seat to take your hand, but she doesn't need to. It is always, in some way, in yours.

'It's time to stop,' she says.

'Yes,' you say, 'it's time to stop.'

There's a street beside you, Justice Walk, which is short and leads directly into town. One day you will go down it. From there, up Bridge Street, across one of the little bridges that hops the River Anker, which sounds far grander than it is. You will walk past the businesses and shops, and for a moment there will be stillness as you remember the chip shop you ran. How your skin was always greasy and your hair smelled of fat and life was simpler, or at least the path ahead was straight.

You will keep walking and hear the clanking poles of market traders building their stalls. It's hard to go into town without bumping into someone who knows all your business. All the friendly 'Hello's and 'How are you?'s All the 'What's Sue up to?' and 'How are your boys getting on?' All the 'I can't imagine what it must have been like,' and the 'I don't know how you survived it,' and the 'Morgan was such a lovely lad.' All these things you know.

Passing the fountain that teenagers fill with bubble bath in the summer, you'll watch the bubbles swell and tear and float away, the last of them making it all the way to Morgan's mural, his smile. His eyes looking out across the town.

Walking down through the market to Pool Bank Street, you'll take a deep breath as you stand on the spot where Morgan staggered after he was stabbed, just before he fell to the ground. Here, on the TV news coverage of his murder, you saw his blood on the pavement and can't forget it. You stand there, right across the street from where the old Co-op Hall used to be, and you're telling the story of what took place on that night five years before to me, as I'm writing this book about what happened to Morgan and your family, when suddenly a young man in a sand-coloured tracksuit passes by on a bike. Your next breath is stolen, then the one after that, then the one after that, because the young man on the bike looks like one of the young men who killed your son.

And then you breathe again, because it wasn't. It was just a young man on a bike. And you carry on. You carry on talking and you carry on walking and you go to his grave and you carry on living because you must. You carry on remembering the town before death howled through it, when life was something else to you. One day soon you will leave, for the sake of your future, at the behest of your past.

The bubbles leave stains on the street.

Know this, Colin. You lost because you couldn't have won. Every department of the institutions designed to protect you will lay claim to changing or having changed, to learning or promising to learn, to not doing things the same way any more, to having been wrong but not being wrong again. You

248

want them to be better, that's all. But you were due better first. Every step of the way it felt to you that the justice system was offender led rather than victim led. From the way the smuggling of weapons into court was kept from the jury, to the allowances the judge gave to the defendants for pleading guilty in the face of overwhelming evidence, to the assumption of rehabilitation awarded to violent offenders on their release despite no evidence of rehabilitation whatsoever, to the months and years you've spent fighting for the truth to be dragged into the light, even when officer after officer was deployed to give you answers that might make you stop asking – answers that should always have been yours. It was always about them.

You'll watch the prime minister, Boris Johnson, proudly announce his government's plans to spend millions on recruiting 20,000 new police officers, and millions more on prison and probation reform, and it'll sound to anyone listening that everything is magically fixed. But you'll know that this same government, in austerity, made sharp, deep cuts to resources in the first place, like in 2010 when spending on youth justice, including projects to reduce knife crime, was cut by 45 per cent, and injuries caused by knife crime rose by 30 per cent. And you will wonder exactly what this means. Whether Morgan's death was part of some social experiment to see if a country can navigate the human cost of under-funded police forces. If that explains cops who don't or can't gather evidence, and their superiors who don't or can't make them. If that makes sense of the dangerous, unwatched men who walk the streets with knives, and the innocent lives they take. Is it collateral, just collateral, of an outmoded, inept and under-resourced system that contorts to protect itself when it fails to protect others? All of this, reported on the same news bulletins as tax loopholes for the super-wealthy, bailed-out banks and a giant *Knife Angel*, its hands turned in anguish to the sky.

A week after your final meeting at the Justice Centre, almost four years after Morgan's death, you'll watch BBC News report that a fifty-two-year-old solicitor, Peter Duncan, has been stabbed to death in Newcastle by a seventeen-year-old boy, Ewan Ireland, who he didn't know. In a brief altercation outside a shopping centre, Mr Duncan had a stolen screwdriver thrust through his heart. Soon they'll discover the boy had seventeen previous convictions for thirty-one offences in the previous two years. That at the time of the murder he was on bail for an offence of affray, was under investigation for a robbery, and still subject to a twelve-month conditional discharge for a battery offence the previous summer. In a Victim Impact Statement read aloud outside Newcastle Crown Court, the solicitor's grieving widow will say that her life 'was ruined by a senseless and unprovoked act. The person who did this had convictions. Nothing stopped him. He continued and he murdered my husband.'

And you will think of Declan Gray. Though you never call him Declan Gray. You always call him Declan. Just Declan. Said with a cold and startling intimacy for someone who is now and always will be a part of your story, though you never wanted him there.

How you yearn not to ask yourself. But you must, and you do. Does he regret it? Does Declan Gray regret killing your son?

You can never know for sure. But you think he must. He didn't get up that morning thinking: today I am going to kill someone. He never thought: today is my last day of freedom before I spend the next twenty-three years of my life in prison.

But you'll always believe he will regret being in prison more. He will regret being caught. Because he never worked out that his actions might one day end a life, even though he had already ended another. He didn't have the ability. He didn't have the empathy that separates him from your son.

Justice without truth is not justice. An apology for the past is not enough. The real regret will always be yours.

It never stops, you know. No matter how much you want it to stop, there will always be more. It'll come as a letter or a phone call, or a knock at the door, but it will always come.

On Christmas Eve 2019, Simon Rowbotham will reach the automatic release point in his sentence for Morgan's manslaughter, as required by law. He'll have served three and a half years of an eight-year term. But his licence will be revoked and he will be recalled to custody just a week later, on New Year's Eve, as a result of concerns about him appearing to be under the influence of illicit substances, which constitutes a clear violation of his parole conditions.

As is required by law, Rowbotham's case will be referred to the Parole Board by the Secretary of State for Justice to determine whether he can be safely released on parole licence again. The case will be considered at an oral hearing on 25 June 2020, conducted via telephone due to the restrictions imposed by the coronavirus pandemic. The panel will only direct release if they are satisfied that it is no longer necessary for the protection of the public that Rowbotham remains confined in prison.

In reaching its decision, the panel will consider the contents of Rowbotham's dossier, prepared by the Secretary of State, take oral evidence from Rowbotham's probation officer based in the community, and the official supervising his case in prison. Rowbotham will also give evidence to the panel.

And you will appear at the hearing too. Kind of. You'll want to be there in person, but the pandemic will put paid to that. Never mind. You'll boot up Skype, and, when directed, just before the main hearing begins, you'll read a new Victim Personal Statement to the panel and a representative of the Secretary of State. And you will say this:

I want Simon to learn from what he has done with his pivotal role in Morgan's death. I miss my son so much, more than I can hate anyone else. I can't fix things that cannot be fixed. I watched the Channel 5 programme after Morgan's death. In this programme, Simon is bragging about his prison background and criminality, helping his criminal friends. It gave me an insight into his world. I really hoped that being in prison this time and released would give Simon a chance of a fresh new start. In a way, by doing that would mean he was not mocking Morgan's death as just another arrest and another bad night out. Morgan doesn't get a chance of a new start or a new life. Simon has got that chance.

The panel will note that your words 'clearly conveyed the devastating impact of Mr Rowbotham's crime and the long consequences of his offending'.

After you've done your bit, you'll be cut off. You won't be present, physically or virtually, when the panel consider the index offences, or the relevant patterns of previous offending and the other evidence before it. You won't be there when the panel list the relevant risk factors, the influences that make it more likely Rowbotham will offend.

At the time of his offending, these risk factors will be said to have included using illegal drugs, problem drinking, not being able to control extreme emotions, antisocial friends, thinking it was acceptable to commit crime, unhelpful ways of thinking and feeling unusually low.

The panel will also hear that Rowbotham has not undertaken accredited programmes to address offending behaviour and his probation officer's recommendation that he needs to undertake work to address his violent offending before release. They will examine the release plan provided by Rowbotham's probation officer and weigh its proposals against the assessed risks. And though the plan will include a requirement to reside in designated accommodation as well as strict limitations on Rowbotham's contacts, movements and activities, they will conclude that this plan is not robust enough to manage Rowbotham in the community at this stage. They will decide that he is not to be granted parole, because he needs to complete programmes to address his violence and decision-making skills before he can safely be rereleased into the community.

They will decide that it isn't safe to release him, even though he already walked out of prison once before, on Christmas Eve 2019, as was his right to do so automatically, by law.

A few weeks after you read out your Victim Personal Statement to Rowbotham's parole hearing over Skype, on an otherwise normal Sunday evening in July 2020, when you're pottering around at home while Sue watches TV in the lounge, you'll receive a phone call from a friend of Morgan's, who will sound a little shaken. You'll ask him what's wrong, and he'll have no choice but to say it. To blurt it out. To let you know what you don't want to hear.

He was walking through the park at the top of Pool Bank Street when he saw a man in a hoodie sitting on a bench. As he got closer, he looked at the man and the man looked back and they both kind of nodded. And then he continued on his way.

He'll say he has no evidence, but he thinks it was Karlton Gray.

Karlton Gray will have reached the automatic release point in his sentence for Morgan's manslaughter, as required by law, in March 2019, having served less than three years of his six years, nine months prison term. One of the conditions of his release on licence is adherence to an exclusion zone that encompasses Nuneaton, Bedworth and the surrounding areas, one large enough to prevent him being anywhere near you or your family, and one that would definitely forbid him from sitting on that bench, in that park, less than 200 yards from where Morgan was murdered. Less than half a mile from the gym where Eamon, now nineteen and preparing to leave Nuneaton for university, goes to work out.

On Wednesday, 22 July 2020 Karlton Gray will be arrested in Whitley Village, Coventry, and recalled to prison for violating the conditions of his licence. Now, like Simon Rowbotham before him, he must sit before a Parole Board to secure release before the end of his sentence, and once again you will give a Victim Personal Statement about the impact of his actions on your family's lives.

You won't feel anything about them being in prison. Not joy. Not pleasure. Not a sense of victory. But you will never understand why they were legally entitled to automatic release less than halfway through their sentences when they had not been rehabilitated. Why, in release, they were granted a freedom that relies upon the goodwill of the offender, despite the offender having demonstrated none.

Sometimes, to escape it all, you'll climb the tallest mountains in Yorkshire, over and over in all kinds of weather. You never used to be a hiker, but now it seems you are. Not just you either, Sue comes too, the pair of you in your boots and coats, walking onwards, always onwards, with Jimmy chasing birds across the rocks. Sometimes you film these climbs, edit them together and set them to music. It doesn't matter that no one else will ever see them but you. It's not about that. It's about the two of you, together, getting almost as far away as it's possible to be.

There's a robin, its red breast tinted orange as it merges with the shimmering, silvery feathers on its side. It comes when you visit Morgan's grave. It perches on the headstone and it watches as you do what has now become tradition. You pour Morgan a nice cold beer into the glass that is always there for him, you take a sip, and you set it down. You used to think the robin was Morgan. Here to see you, to keep you company, to reassure you that in some way he lives on. But you don't think that any more. Morgan hasn't taken the form of a bird. That robin just wants food. He's hoping you'll tidy the grass on Morgan's grave and find a nice juicy worm for him to eat.

You don't look for signs any more, because there are none. They are as futile as a dream he'll return. And now you no longer cling to false hope, you feel freer than you did before. You don't search for God because you know he is not there. You and your family are alone. If you and the robin share anything, it's a desire to provide the best for them. A fat, juicy worm of your own.

You'll always struggle, though. You know that. You and Sue and Connor and Eamon. You'll always struggle. There are two lives now: the one lived and the one not, what has been and what could have been. You'll exist in the void between them. Everything good it is possible to experience exists there with you. Joy. Love. Pride. Serenity. Inspiration. Gratitude. Awe. It exists, but it is split in two.

When you're asked what life is like after your son is murdered, you'll smile and answer honestly.

'It is shit.'

But you're together, you and Sue. Thirty years you've been married, though you're no longer the couple who exchanged vows. She says she believes you're cursed. That you have to be. It's the only thing that could possibly make sense. And there is no way to argue with that is there, really? Not with someone who is always right. Because now you are a wife who is at best doing OK, and at worst very sad for long, long stretches of time, and you are a husband who can't hope to understand the way she's feeling, because you barely understand yourself. You're an island divided in two by a flood, the roots of your trees still tangled underwater.

Sometimes you think about a couple you once saw on TV. The wife had been badly disfigured in an accident. Her handsome husband was by her side, holding her hand, saying he married the person inside her, that the person inside her is the one he loves. It's not like that for you and Sue. You both look the same on the outside. A little more tired, maybe. Deeper lines around sadder eyes. But you look just like any ordinary Nuneaton couple. Except you're not. It's your insides that are changed.

You're not the victims, though. The victim was always your son.

Morgan's bass guitar sits on a stand in the corner of the lounge. Sometimes you look at it. Sometimes you pick it up. Sometimes you pluck the strings and feel the notes move through you. Onwards along an endless road, there is distance, but he gets no further away.

Epilogue

Saturday, 31 June 2018

It's hot. Sticky hot. Furnace hot. Stepping-off-a-plane-in-a-foreign-country hot. Not ideal for Irish skin, that's for sure. But not one of you stops working. Not one of you will rest until this is done.

Trey builds the walls, and before they're even finished, you and Sue and Tam and Helen and Jodie are lifting the giant canvases out of the van to hang them. Before long, the room at the CAVA centre down by Nuneaton train station is transformed, and all around you are photographs of Morgan's graffiti, a trail of paint like the one he left behind him. The first exhibition in his name. It makes perfect sense he'll be remembered in colour, on a wall, with everyone looking at him and smiling.

Years ago, when you first bought the DSLR camera, you knew Morgan would want to run away with it and claim it as his own. He'd expressed an interest in photography that had bloomed with his love of graffiti. It seemed the perfect way of preserving his art and his memories of making it, before the inevitable happened and it was all scrubbed clean. You wanted to encourage this – his eyes got even brighter whenever the topic came up – so you told him he could share it. But first he had to put some of his own birthday money into buying it. That way, he knew he was responsible for it too, and then maybe he wouldn't smash it up, the way he did every phone he ever owned.

You got the beers in and his friends came over one night a few months back – Craig, Trey, Kyle, Dave and Joe – and you spent the night going through Morgan's photographs of his GRUT tag, each choosing some to blow up for the exhibition from the hundreds he had taken. This was important. You didn't want it to become a proud-dad display. You didn't want it to be wishy-washy, or even sentimental. You didn't want it to be about you. You wanted it to be about GRUT.

You open the doors to the exhibition, and people come to see his art. They stand in front of the canvases and they see his tag, and they smile to themselves and thank you and say you should be proud. (Which you should be. You should be. It looks really cool, doesn't it? It just looks really cool.) You are. You are proud. You always will be.

Days, weeks, months, years later, when they travel somewhere, these people, when they go on holiday, when they're out living their lives, they will remember it. They will write it on a lamp-post in Santorini, Greece. They will spell it out in rocks on an Ibizan beach. They will paint it on a coconut in Xelha, Mexico. They will spray it large in silver on a Barcelona wall.

GRUT.

It does mean something after all. It means he is there.

Acknowledgements

Thank you to Colin, Sue, Connor and Eamon Hehir for sharing everything you've shared with me and in these pages. Thank you for your openness, your kindness and your friendship. Your family has always been remarkable.

Thank you to Claire Harrison, Nuneaton's Lois Lane, for thinking of me in the beginning, being there in the middle, and always replying in under five seconds even at the end.

Thank you to my editor and publisher, Francesca Main. I am extremely lucky to get to work with you, and to count you as a friend. I'm glad someone knows what they're doing.

Thank you to my agent Cathryn Summerhayes, for everything as ever.

Thank you to everyone at Phoenix and Orion.

Thank you to Michael Gillard, Amanda Davis, Jess Molloy, The Society of Authors and the Authors' Foundation.

Thank you to my old Nuneaton friends, Jonothon Lees, John Talbot, Daniel Shaw, Nadeem Deen and Adam Street, for their help remembering and the decades of nonsense.

Love to my family, Mum, Dad, Glenn, Alison, Darren, Alex, William, Oliver, Thomas, Anna, Jonathan and the Jakemans.

Lou, Douglas and Elmer, I love you.

Credits

Phoenix would like to thank everyone at Orion who worked on the publication of *About A Son*.

Agent
Cathryn Summerhayes

Editor
Francesca Main

Copy-editor
Linden Lawson

Proofreader
Clare Hubbard

Editorial Management
Rosie Pearce
Kate Moreton
Jane Hughes
Charlie Panayiotou
Tamara Morriss
Claire Boyle

Audio
Paul Stark
Jake Alderson
Georgina Cutler

Contracts
Anne Goddard
Ellie Bowker
Humayra Ahmed

Design
Steve Marking
Nick Shah
Joanna Ridley
Helen Ewing

Inventory
Jo Jacobs
Dan Stevens

Finance
Nick Gibson
Jasdip Nandra
Elizabeth Beaumont
Ibukun Ademefun
Afeera Ahmed
Sue Baker
Tom Costello

Marketing
Tom Noble

Production
Hannah Cox
Fiona McIntosh

Publicity
Francesca Pearce

Sales
Jen Wilson
Victoria Laws
Esther Waters
Frances Doyle
Ben Goddard
Jack Hallam
Anna Egelstaff
Inês Figueira
Barbara Ronan

Andrew Hally
Dominic Smith
Deborah Deyong
Lauren Buck
Maggy Park
Linda McGregor
Sinead White
Jemimah James
Rachael Jones
Jack Dennison
Nigel Andrews
Ian Williamson
Julia Benson
Declan Kyle
Robert Mackenzie
Megan Smith
Charlotte Clay
Rebecca Cobbold

Operations
Sharon Willis

Rights
Susan Howe
Krystyna Kujawinska
Jessica Purdue
Ayesha Kinley
Louise Henderson